# BOWL LIKE A PRO

## DAVID OZIO
### with DAN HERBST

CB
CONTEMPORARY
BOOKS
CHICAGO

**Library of Congress Cataloging-in-Publication Data**

Ozio, David.
    Bowl like a pro : winning techniques and strategies that will
raise your average / David Ozio with Dan Herbst.
      p.   cm.
    Includes index.
    ISBN 0-8092-4039-4
    1. Bowling.   I. Herbst, Dan.   II. Title.
GV903.095   1992
794.6—dc20                          92-11488
                                                    CIP

Published by Contemporary Books, Inc.
Two Prudential Plaza, Chicago, Illinois 60601-6790
Manufactured in the United States of America
International Standard Book Number: 0-8092-4039-4

# Contents

# *Preface*

For more than 20 years the attempt to overcome the sheer challenge that bowling represents has been my mission. As I write this my career is going well, although I have yet to realize several goals. At the top of my wish list is a desire to complete the Triple Crown (by winning the U.S. Open and the PBA National) and to bowl well enough to be considered for the Hall of Fame.

I'm sure that you also have bowling goals. They might not seem as glamorous as those that we pros harbor but that doesn't make them any less difficult to achieve. It's my hope that the experience and knowledge that I have gained in the sport will be reflected in the pages ahead so that you will obtain the competitive edge that you need to fulfill your potential.

The constant striving to improve is what makes this game so enjoyable for me. I still recall how I felt as a 16-year-old who kept score for my dad. I spent countless hours watching him bowl at Village Lanes in our hometown, Beaumont. My father was a good player who made the game seem easy, at least to his son's eyes.

His success inspired me to give bowling a try. But I soon discovered that what had appeared easy was anything but. I found it annoying and very frustrating that my initial performances couldn't meet my expectations. My pride was hurt. My athletic ability had been challenged.

The desire to prove to myself that I could master this game as my dad had seemingly done was what spurred me to practice with an attitude that approached an all-encompassing passion. It was that same pride that would later prevent me from quitting the PBA Tour after several years in which I had every right to think that I just wasn't good enough to compete with the greatest players in the world.

Through my first six full years on the Tour I didn't win a title. After entering 160 events I had earned a mere $106,482 on a circuit in which a week on the road costs about $750. Clearly, my apprenticeship had been anything but satisfying.

But I knew that to quit would mean that bowling had beaten me. So I kept plugging away, and in 1985 I won two titles. I finished 11th in earnings that year with $85,100. I have placed among the top 20 every year since, except 1988, including enjoying something of a fantasy year in 1991 when I was named Player and Bowler of the Year. Those honors followed four wins, including the Firestone Tournament of Champions.

I had always thought that such a run would represent the pinnacle to me. But it didn't. I still have many ambitions to meet. I hope that when my career ends I can look back at 1991 as a stepping stone and not as a brief moment in the sun.

To win the Firestone was a great feeling, given that the field consists exclusively of PBA champions. But, to me, another victory was even more satisfying. My most emotional triumph came at Boulevard Bowl in Edmond, Oklahoma, in 1988. That center is run by Richard Altman, who was also my sponsor at the time. I had to strike out in the 10th frame to defeat Del Warren 236–235 in a match in which I had trailed by 21 pins. To do so in front of a national TV audience in my sponsor's bowling center still ranks as a moment of tremendous satisfaction. For those few late frames, at least, I had overcome the challenge that was first put to me by Elwood Ozio in the late 1960s.

Which brings us back to this book. To have been asked to author it was a nice compliment. I have long heard that I possess the so-called classic bowling style. It's my hope that you can put the advice I'm about to offer to full use.

I have always been mystified that very few bowlers emulate their golfing and tennis brethren by seeking out pros for lessons. Because of the lack of demand, there are only a handful of teaching pros who make their living helping others. That means that you, the bowler, must rely more than your counterparts in other sports on books and videos.

Both my writer, Dan Herbst, and I have put a lot of time, thought, and effort into trying to fulfill our mandate to make you a better player. Let me caution you that no advice by itself, regardless of how valid it might be, can turn a 150-average player into a scratch shooter. However, if you take our words to heart and commit yourself to countless hours of practice, you should become a far better bowler.

I wish you lots of luck. And I hope that your efforts meet with the same sense of satisfaction as you pursue your bowling goals as I have enjoyed while pursuing mine.

David Ozio

***Coauthor Dan Herbst (left) with David Ozio.*** Dan Chidester

# Introduction

Since far back in our collective history, human beings have attempted to knock over objects with balls, and the various forms of bowling have evolved considerably ever since Rip Van Winkle's day.

Tenpins has become the most common variety, although it has several relatives. Bowls and boccie involve rolling a bigger ball next to a small target one. Candlepin bowling allows up to three attempts per frame for the contestant to propel a softball-sized sphere at 10 very thin sticks.

One thing that has remained constant is that very few of us are often satisfied with our performances. One can almost picture early man kicking the side of the cave in disgust after blowing an easy shot.

Many players' shortcomings—both then and now—can be rectified. In the pages ahead, one of the greatest stars on the Professional Bowlers Association Tour will offer suggestions on how you can improve your game. David Ozio's pointers are aimed primarily at the majority of today's participants. He hopes to help you elevate your average above its current plateau.

We have tried to keep things as straightforward as possible. Bowling isn't complex, but neither is it as simple as its critics sometimes suggest. As with all of your endeavors, knowledge is the key. Toward that end, Dave will address what you should be doing and offer suggestions about pitfalls that you must avoid.

Ozio possesses excellent credentials for this task. Not only is he respected by his peers as a consummate student of the game, he's also a highly articulate individual who spends a great deal of his time interacting with amateur bowlers. He has gained a deserved reputation as one of the hardest-working players on the Tour by virtue of his tireless practice habits.

Many knowledgeable observers consider Ozio's style the one to emulate. His delivery is smooth and devoid of superfluous movement. By combining square shoulders with an ideal pendulum armswing and virtually flawless timing, David Ozio has become a top star.

Like all PBA Touring players, Dave participates in the Pro-Am segments that precede every national tournament stop. He's had the opportunity to bowl with—and observe firsthand—tens of thousands of lower- and middle-average players. He has offered his amateur partners tips on what flaws they must eliminate to enjoy greater success.

Dave now puts his observations on paper so that you can gain the same benefits as those who pay a lot more money for the privilege of competing in a PBA Pro-Am event. It is our hope that the pages ahead start you on your way to becoming a better player so that you will derive more satisfaction and fun from your trips to the lanes.

As for Dave's track record, it can truly be said to be top shelf. His most prestigious victory came in 1991 when he captured professional bowling's most coveted crown, the Firestone Tournament of Champions. Rolling strikes in eight of the first nine frames of the title game, Ozio over-

***The author is shown
en route to winning
the 1991 Firestone
Tournament of
Champions.*** Russ Vitale

whelmed reigning two-time Player of the Year Amleto Monacelli 236–203.

Dave's greatest triumph was made even more memorable by the events of April 27, 1991. Prior to the nationally televised title round, a bomb threat was received. The bowling center was evacuated while millions of TV viewers were treated to interviews with the finalists that were conducted live from the parking lot.

After a lengthy delay and much confusion, everyone was ushered back inside. An extensive search uncovered that the only explosives at Riviera Lanes were located inside Ozio's bowling ball. In the semifinal game Dave put on a striking exhibition as he eliminated Mike Miller 240–227 to earn his title game berth.

Ozio's triumph came only weeks after celebrating his 37th birthday. It has helped to cement what must be a virtually certain future induction into bowling's Hall of Fame.

In 1991, Ozio became a member of an elite group of PBA standouts who have claimed 10 or more national Tour victories. At the same time, he virtually clinched 1991 Player of the Year honors when he won the Chevy Truck Classic in dramatic fashion.

With the Player of the Year race up for grabs among several outstanding candidates, Ozio coasted past Marc McDowell 235–160 in the championship match. To reach that contest Ozio had to demonstrate his ice-cool nerve in pressure situations during the final frames of the semifinal contest.

Opponent Bryan Goebel had concluded his activities with a 244 score. With a capacity crowd in Rochester, New York, and a national television audience watching (and with

**Ozio toppled 910 pins in four games during the championship round of the prestigious 1990 American Bowling Congress Masters Tournament.** Courtesy of American Bowling Congress

a chance at the $27,000 top prize on the line), Ozio calmly deposited three consecutive shots in the pocket. Having struck out, he secured a thrilling come-from-behind win by a two-pin margin.

Less than two months later it was official: Ozio was selected by his peers as 1991's top bowler. David was cited by 82 percent of the ballots; he garnered 1,083 out of 1,320 votes. John Mazza, with 99 votes, finished second.

Ozio's 1991 statistics are a testimony to his greatness. On a circuit in which only one out of three tournament entries receives a check, he cashed in 24 out of 32 attempts. In 16 of those events he was one of two dozen players out of the typical 160-player field who qualified for the match play segment of the tournament. David's 215.64 average was fourth best on the Tour.

He was at his best during big occasions. Ozio placed among the top five players in three of pro bowling's "big four" events. In addition to his Tournament of Champions triumph, Ozio was fourth in the PBA National Championship, and he finished fifth at the American Bowling Congress Masters.

David Ozio's official yearly earnings of $225,585 was nearly half again better than that of his closest pursuer. Since the PBA's start in 1959, only Mike Aulby has ever eclipsed that figure in a calendar year.

Ozio gave notice early on that 1991 was to be his year. During the Winter Tour he paced the pros for most money earned and championship round winning percentage among those with five or more games (6–1/.857). He tied with Pete Weber for the most titles.

Ozio began by capturing back-to-back tournaments. He ended 1991 by bowling his 13th career PBA perfect game during play in the Cambridge Mixed Doubles Championship.

David's 1991 blitz started with a 259–225 defeat of Walter Ray Williams at the AC-Delco Classic. That was followed by a conquest of Miller at the Showboat Invitational 279–224. Ozio thus joined Hall of Fame members Dick

Weber and Don Johnson as the only men to begin a year with consecutive victories.

Early during the Spring Tour Ozio became the 14th player in PBA history to win over $150,000 in a single year. His 1991 showing marked the sixth time in seven years that the popular Texan had finished among the PBA's top 20 earners.

Married to Lisa, Dave is the father of Heather and Haleigh.

Dan Herbst

# 1
# *The Basics of Bowling*

During a rare slump, legendary Green Bay Packers head coach Vince Lombardi decided it was time for his team to get back to fundamentals. Standing in front of the perennial champions, he held his arm aloft and dryly announced, "This, gentlemen, is a football." From the back of the room came the voice of Max McGee, the team's wittiest player. "Hold it, coach," McGee pleaded. "You're going too fast!"

Since I'm not strong enough to hold a bowling ball above my head for any length of time, I will assume that you already have some basic knowledge about the sport. I trust that you are able to keep score or at least bowl with someone who does or in a center whose computers do the math for you. I wish only to offer pointers on how you can improve your ability to knock over pins.

Like Lombardi, let's begin at the beginning. That round object can weigh up to a legal maximum of 16 pounds. With rare exceptions, it features three openings, a hole apiece for your thumb, middle, and ring fingers. Unless you have wrists made of iron—à la Mike Miller—it's a very good idea to make use of the thumbhole. Mike is one

**Mike Miller's unorthodox thumbless grip has helped to make him a star, but it's not a technique for the masses.** Russ Vitale

in a million, and his thumbless success is something that you can imitate only by risking injury.

Few games are as simple as bowling. Your chore is no more complex than to knock over 10 pieces of wood that are placed in a triangular configuration 60 feet away. So basic is this objective that children can bowl—with some help from Mom, Dad, or an older sibling—almost as soon as they can walk.

The beauty of bowling is that it's possible for you to enjoy it on so many levels. Walk into a center and you can find players who run the gamut from strictly recreational to seriously competitive. The rawest of beginners can roll a strike, while even the greatest of the pros is occasionally snakebitten by a gutter ball.

This range of skill is both bowling's greatest selling point and its biggest detriment. Since anyone can play, it's among the most popular of participatory sports. But because everyone can enjoy that singular game in which everything falls into place, there is nowhere near the amount of respect granted to the sport's top performers that they deserve.

It is one thing for an average Joe to roll a 230 game. It's quite another matter for people to assume that means that Joe could have beaten a top pro during those 10 frames. We pros roll on lane conditions that are as different from those of the typical center as the famed Augusta National is from a miniature golf course. But, unlike in golf, one can't visibly discern the tremendous differences between the oil pattern at your local center and those found on the Professional Bowlers Association (PBA) Tour.

The very incorrect assumption made by many is that bowling is a great recreational activity that's not quite a legitimate competitive endeavor. To bowl at the highest levels is very demanding, both physically and mentally. To reach the televised title round in most tournaments requires rolling as many as 30 games in a two-day span.

The typical professional tournament has us bowl three blocks in qualifying rounds of six games apiece. The field is then cut to the top 24. During a 36-hour period the remaining pros roll three blocks of eight match games in which the winner of each match receives 30 bonus pins.

Only after all that are the five players determined who have earned the right to bowl on television for the title and big money. While it's certainly nice to pick up a check with several zeroes and a comma in it, the bottom line is that two out of three entrants do not cash, and 155 of the typical 160-player field do not make it to the title round.

Prize money is intentionally top-heavy. You have to be good to make a good living as a professional bowler. In fact, you have to be very good. There are a lot of extremely gifted players who are "sent home" when they discover just how tough it is to survive on a Tour in which one must earn approximately $25,000 a year just to break even.

Happily, not everyone who bowls faces such odds.

Those of us who love to compete enjoy the challenge. It's up to you to decide for yourself what neighborhood—recreational or competitive—you wish to inhabit. You can enjoy bowling as a fun night out with some friends or as a chance to test yourself athletically. Or perhaps a combination of both.

Go into any center at peak hours and you will likely see all colors of the bowling spectrum, ranging from a young child's birthday party up to adults who are battling with the same seriousness as would athletes in any other sport.

Most bowlers fall somewhere between these two extremes. The beauty of bowling is that you can compete and converse. You can play to win while sharing a laugh. And you can work to improve while safe in the knowledge that a bad shot won't end up in the woods or buried in sand.

Bowling is fun. But like any game in which a score is kept, it sure is more enjoyable when you do it well. I hope you can find a balance between wanting to do your best and enjoying the time you spend on the lanes. Even at the professional level, bowling should always be fun no matter how great the pressure to perform might become. Among beginners, bowling should represent a challenge in which you do care about becoming more proficient at toppling pins.

Your first assignment concerns lane geography. Oil patterns can vary widely. While all alleys are standardized, they're far from identical. Some lanes tend to help make bowling balls hook a lot, others retard hook. Some pins are relatively easy to knock over while others fall only with a stinginess that would please Ebenezer Scrooge.

Whether you do your bowling in a house that's easy or one that's difficult, there are some things you can be certain of. The headpin will be 60 feet from the foul line and equidistant from the two gutters. The weight of each pin will fall within the American Bowling Congress's prescribed range of 3 pounds and 6 ounces up to 3 pounds and 10 ounces. Heavier pins last longer but lighter wood usually results in better scoring.

## LANE GEOGRAPHY

The traditional lane consists of stripes of wood that are placed in one-inch-wide boards. They run from the approach to just in front of the pins. The segment of each lane between the foul line and the arrows—known as the head portion—consists of maple. A hard-surface wood, maple is best able to absorb the impact of a succession of shots. The remainder of the lane is made from pine. The exceptions are the modern synthetic surfaces.

Either way, there are seven arrows on every lane. These are not decorative items. They're found at intervals of one every five boards. For purposes of easy identification, they're numbered from one to seven. The first arrow—which is five boards in from the gutter—is on the far right side of the lane for a right-handed player or the far left side for you southpaws.

The second arrow—found on board number 10—is on

**Right-handed league bowler Laurie Rodman uses the second arrow as her aiming point.** Dan Chidester

the same board as the 6 pin (for righties) or the 4 pin (lefties). The third arrow is on the 15th board, the same plank as the 3 pin (righties) or the 2 pin (lefties). The center arrow corresponds with the middle of the headpin.

You will find a series of dots on the approach and another along the foul line. These, too, exist to help with your aiming process. These serve as guides on which you align your feet.

The arrows are a great help. Many lower-average players make the mistake of using the pins as their target, or they look straight down as they release the ball. The arrows are just far enough away to force you to keep your head steady during your entire delivery, yet are sufficiently close as to be less difficult to hit.

A steady head is a vital but often overlooked ingredient in good bowling. It's been said that Marshall Holman's noggin is so steady throughout his delivery that you could probably put a cup of water up there without spilling a drop.

Why aim at the arrows when it's the pins you wish to hit? Think of it this way: you're at a carnival and the three-balls-for-a-dollar game has two baskets. One basket is 60 feet away and the other is 15 feet away. Which do you think gives you a better chance at taking home that big stuffed giraffe on the top shelf?

Some players use the dots on the foul line or just beyond it as their target. While it is possible to be successful with such an approach, I don't recommend it. As you walk forward during your delivery process, your head must drop downward to keep your eye on the dots. This contradicts one of the key principles of bowling: that a steady head is required to get steady results.

As with all bowling "rules," there are some exceptions. Pete Weber and Mike Edwards use the dots for guidance. However, neither bobs his head during his approach. That's an amazing combination. Chances are that using a target that's too close will cause your head to move during your delivery.

Moreover, a close target makes it tempting to drop your shot. It can also cause you to bend excessively at the waist, which in turn will cause you to project the ball into the lane and/or decrease your leverage.

By trying to roll your ball over an arrow you will be encouraged to follow through—and keep your eyes on your target. The majority of better players use the arrows as their targets. You should, too.

Through trial and error you will discover how moving your feet or your target or both will change where the ball will impact when it reaches the pin deck. Later we will study the advantages of cross-lane spare shooting. We will also discuss playing the various strike angles, which range from the gutter to the deep inside line. All of these concepts are made possible by the presence of the arrows and the dots.

In the process, you will learn a new language. In the paddock (locker room) during a PBA event it's not unusual to hear a player declare, "I was on 30 bellying it right early banking it out to three with creep speed."

Translated into English, this means that this right-handed bowler was standing well to the left of center of the lane, about 35 boards from the right gutter (a left-handed player would be found on the far right side of the approach). He was releasing his shots at that 30th board (which corresponds with the sixth arrow and is near the left gutter), and sending it sideways. Our bowler was trying to get his ball into the dry section of the lane quickly. He was aiming far to the right with his shot going out as far as the third board.

*Creep speed,* as you probably guessed, is when your ball moves about as slowly as a 95-year-old motorist (conversely, *rocket speed* is 20 mph, with Eugene McCune's 30-mph spare ball being to the best of my knowledge the fastest on record).

The term *bellying* means to play a deep inside line. You stand far to the opposite side of your bowling hand to allow for a great amount of hook, projecting your shot

***Ozio's address and release positions while playing an
inside line.*** Dan Chidester

toward the gutter before it begins its hooking motion toward the pocket.

On other occasions, you may decide to *point it up.* You
will stand by the gutter that's on the same side of the lane
as your bowling hand (right-handed players to the right,
lefties to the left). The ball will roll almost on a straight
line to the pocket with only the most modest amount of
hook used.

Or you might opt to *play the gutter.* The ball rolls
alongside the channel before it breaks toward the pocket.
If you think you have a strong stomach, try playing that
line, in which the slightest of mistakes results in a gutter
ball that could prevent you from winning a major tournament.

***Ozio's address and release positions while playing the gutter.*** Dan Chidester

To play the gutter means to risk potential embarrassment. Given the ever-so-slight margin for error, the difference between rolling that crucial clutch strike or suffering bowling's ultimate humiliation is often no more than an inch.

One of the all-too-rare occasions in which the results of a PBA tournament gained great national media exposure was when Del Ballard, Jr., suffered a gutter ball on his final shot to lose the title game of the 1991 Fair Lanes Open to Pete Weber 213–207. That one shot cost Del the $14,500 differential between first and second place, not to mention unrelenting ribbing from his fellow pros.

Those in the media who reported that Del "choked" were mistaken. He had just produced two picture perfect

**Contrary to popular misrepresentation, Del Ballard's famous gutter ball mishap was not the result of "choking."**
Courtesy of Professional Bowlers Association

strikes in the 10th frame when nothing less would do. And Del is certainly among the tour's finer pressure performers. Often forgotten is how he rolled games of 250 and 223 two weeks later to win the Leisure's Long Island Open.

Nor was Del having fallen victim to the so-called blue board unique. I rolled no less than 23 gutter balls during my quest to win my sport's most prestigious and lucrative title while I competed at the 1991 Firestone Tournament of Champions. Here I was trying to gain the $50,000 top prize and my first major title only to sacrifice hundreds of pins

needlessly. Or so it must have seemed to the casual ob-
server.

But I knew that my best line to the pocket, the one that
would offer the greatest strike-carry percentage, involved
risk taking. Despite all those zeroes, I left Akron victorious.
To play the edge successfully you have to be fearless. If you
fudge your shot to avoid the gutter you are inviting disaster.
Like a tightrope walker, you must concentrate upon successfully completing the task at hand. Distractions, be they
in the form of a 70-foot drop or the gutter, must never be
allowed to enter your mind.

That's another reason why I feel strongly that bowling—when it is done right by serious players—is every bit
as much a legitimate individual sport test as is tennis, golf,
swimming, or boxing. Yes, anyone can bowl poorly.
Anyone can also play basketball or baseball poorly too.

## THE INGREDIENTS OF SUCCESS

To become a top-notch bowler you will need the same level
of natural ability, dedication, and determination that would
bring you to the top of any other sport.

Different lane conditions demand different strike
lines. It does sometimes seem that "all roads lead to Rome"
and to the pocket. Although you can use a wide variety of
angles and degrees of hook to get your ball into that desired zone, pin carry and your margin of error are other
matters.

Professional and top-level amateur bowlers are constantly searching to find the optimum combination of line,
ball type, speed, break point, and hand release that will
give us the greatest amount of leeway. Having a comfort
cushion pays dividends when one's less-than-perfect shots
are still rewarded as strikes. The player who puts up an *X*
after barely missing his target and who can carry those
half-hits enjoys a great competitive edge.

To become a truly outstanding bowler you will need to
learn a lot more than just how to throw the ball. You must
to be able to read lanes, to alter shot speed, to change hand

positions and release points, and to play a wide variety of angles on your strike shots. You will also need to be calm under pressure while possessing sufficient knowledge to be your own coach.

You must also learn how best to deal with your major opponent: yourself.

To reach your full potential, you must become physically fit. The majority of top pros engage in extensive conditioning regimens. Most do a lot of running because we're only as good as our legs.

For now, just working on the basics should prove to be a sufficient challenge. You need to spend a few moments studying the lane map on the facing page. There will be several references later in this book as to which board to stand on and which arrow to aim for when attempting specific spare conversions.

## THE FUNDAMENTALS OF GOOD SHOT MAKING

Regardless of what shot you are trying to execute, certain fundamentals apply to all deliveries. The most important step that you can take as a relative beginner is to become fundamentally sound. For now, forget about your average. If you have been bowling for any appreciable period of time you have probably developed several habits, both good and bad. To keep the former while breaking the latter will not be easy. You may need to sacrifice short-term scoring to achieve long-term improvement.

That is why I suggest that any changes you wish to make in your game should be done between bowling seasons. It can be very frustrating to have your scores go south in league play. Instead, take those few summer months and try to practice at least twice a week. If possible, roll a minimum of three games during each session. Concentrate on areas of your game that need improvement. Don't worry at all about keeping score.

As someone who gives dozens of clinics annually, I have ample opportunity to observe the low-average player.

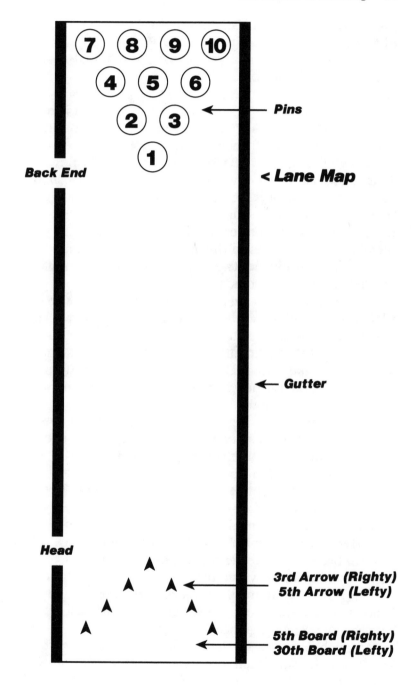

Pins

Back End

< *Lane Map*

Gutter

Head

3rd Arrow (Righty)
5th Arrow (Lefty)

5th Board (Righty)
30th Board (Lefty)

I've noticed that a lot of bowlers in the 120–160 range are hindered by one or two major flaws. Perhaps it's a circuitous armswing, that bobbing head, or bad timing. In many cases, it's simply lack of knowledge where and how to play certain shots.

The good news is that most of you have the potential for vast improvement if you can identify your major problem areas and make the needed corrections.

As you watch the PBA or LPBT (Ladies Pro Bowlers Tour) telecasts, I'm sure you have noticed that, like snowflakes, no two bowlers are exactly alike. I can't think of any other game in which such a wide variety of styles are represented on the professional level. It may seem that there are no style rules to which you must conform.

In a way, that's true. The saying in bowling is that what counts isn't how, but how many. However, the closer you are to the right how, the easier will become the how many half of the equation. While you can become good with an unorthodox style, the simpler your movements, the easier it is to repeat them shot after shot. That ability to achieve repetition is the one quality that all of the leading pros possess. That holds true whether one takes three, four, five, or more steps during the delivery.

Your consistency in repeating a series of motions is vital regardless of your style of play. As with other sports, there is a trade-off one must endure between power and accuracy. Home run hitters, by nature, tend to get on base less often and strike out a lot more than do singles hitters. So, too, in tenpins.

The guys with tremendous power are more susceptible to suffering splits, which leads to more open frames. The control players have fewer opens but don't possess nearly as much carrying power to turn a light hit into a strike.

In bowling parlance, *crankers* or *twisters* are players who impart tremendous hooking action on their shots. Power, not accuracy, is their primary forte.

Straight shooters are the bowlers who rely far more on being accurate for their success. These "down and in" players roll a relatively direct ball.

The third category consists of *strokers* or *tweeners.* (They fall between these two extremes, hence the descriptive term.) My definition of a stroker is a bowler who can combine power and accuracy in a fluid package. Strokers have more power than the straight players and are more accurate than the crankers. The flip side is that they have less power than the crankers and less accuracy than do straight players.

The modern game has seen a greater emphasis on rolling strikes with less reward for making shots. To excel today a player must combine a shot that hits like Mike Tyson but is as accurate as a Larry Bird jump shot. Great players have both attributes. Good ones have a large dose of one and at least a modicum of the other.

While the power-vs.-accuracy issue is a matter of individual preference, the greatest stars in bowling history have all been fundamentally sound. They might have had one unorthodox feature in their style but they performed virtually all of the basic skills by the book.

With rare exceptions, their timing—the relationship between the shot's release vis-à-vis the opposite foot's slide—is consistent. Their armswings are straight and their eyes remain riveted to their target throughout their deliveries. Their bodies are square to the foul line at the point of release. And their wrist is locked into the same position throughout the armswing and follow-through.

With that in mind, let's examine the basic components of a good shot.

## WHEN IT'S YOUR TURN

When it's your turn to bowl you should be ready. There's nothing more annoying to your fellow players than to have to sit around waiting as you return from the snack bar or chat on the telephone. Common courtesy is an important part of allowing all to enjoy their evening.

Speaking of courtesy, bowling etiquette requires that you wait for the players on adjoining lanes to complete their deliveries before you begin yours. Check to either side to make sure you have clearance. If two players step up

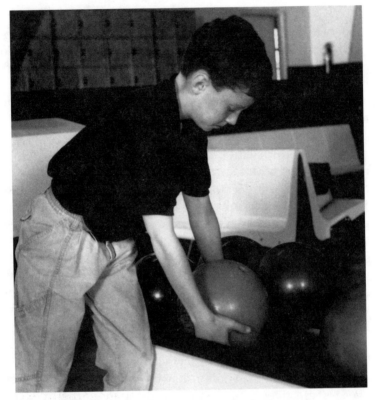

***The right way to remove a ball from the rack.***
Dan Chidester

simultaneously, the bowler on the right has the right-of-way. If others nearby aren't set to start, you should be ready to take your turn. Slow bowling makes it difficult to get into and remain in a good groove.

Obviously, gaining clearance is a safety step designed to avoid collisions. Toward that end, make certain that any body language you employ to "encourage" pins to fall is confined to your own lane.

Having made certain that the coast is clear, your initial step, simple as it sounds, is to remove your ball from the rack. There are a few safety pointers to consider.

First, do not place your fingers anywhere near the exit area where the ball is returned. That wheel that propels the

***The wrong way to remove a ball from the rack.***
Dan Chidester

ball upward can cause serious injury, especially if it grabs hold of a loose bracelet or chain. Wait until your ball is well clear before placing your hands near it.

Second, do not put your fingers into the ball to lift it out of the rack. Doing so would subject your wrist, tendons, and lower back to more pressure than they can safely handle. If you do a lot of bowling you could suffer a needless injury. In addition, should you place your fingers into the ball they could become jammed were another ball to bang into them.

Instead, place your hands on the side of the ball (as

shown in the photo on page 16) to remove the ball from the rack. By placing your hands on the two sides of the ball that are not contacting the other balls you will lessen the likelihood of a mishap.

As you step onto the approach, rub your sliding foot on the lane. This is a precaution used to detect whether any foreign substance might be attached to the bottom of your shoe. The time to discover that you stepped in a soda or a catsup spill or on a stray piece of gum is when you're standing still, not as you're sliding. I've heard horror stories of nasty injuries suffered when players were sent for unexpected flights over the foul line.

If your shoe needs cleaning, put the ball down and perform the necessary steps to ensure your safety. It's possible to bowl for years without this happening, but why take chances? The good habit of testing your shoes' soles before every shot might pay dividends only once. But that one time could mean the difference between a strike or a foul and between maintaining your good health and suffering an injury.

## THE ADDRESS POSITION

Using the dots as your guide, place your sliding foot on the board that you have selected. How far away from the foul line should you stand? That depends on a number of factors such as how many steps you plan to take during your delivery and your size.

Obviously, taller players with longer legs need far more room than I do. Those of you who use five strides will require more space than the handful of players who use a three-step delivery.

Before you roll that first shot you must determine your starting position. Stand on the foul line with your back to the pins. Take one half-step followed by the same number of brisk strides toward the settee area for every step you plan on taking during your delivery (e.g., four-step players take four and a half steps). You have discovered the proper distance that your starting position should be from the foul line.

**The correct address position.** Dan Chidester

After stepping onto the approach and lining up your feet you should cradle the ball in your nonbowling arm. Next, place your fingers into the holes. Always put your ring and middle fingers into the ball first, followed by your thumb. This helps to promote a consistent grip to help you achieve a more consistent release.

As you assume the address position your nonbowling hand works to support the weight of the ball. The ball should be held near your side as shown in the accompanying photo. Note that the bowler on the left is incorrectly holding the ball in the middle of her upper body. That

*During your address do not hold the ball in front of the middle of your body . . .*

*. . . or too high.*
Dan Chidester

means that she will have to swing the ball around her hips on her backswing instead of having the ball move in a straight plane.

The proper starting position helps to execute the ideal armswing. A relatively straight swing is one of the major keys to good shot making. The height at which you hold the ball is up to you. Like most players, I begin with the ball just above my belt. With my eyes and concentration on my target, I am now ready to begin my delivery.

Is it absolutely vital that your armswing be straight? Peter Hakim, who upset Mike Aulby 267–246 during the championship round on his way to winning the 1986 Long Island Open, likes to joke that his game features a "weather vane" armswing. "It goes north, south, east, and west," he explains with a laugh.

Peter isn't the only pro who defies conventional wisdom in this area. Scott Devers is another left-handed player who has enjoyed great success with an armswing that wraps behind his back and is powered by his muscles. Ron Williams actually holds his elbow below and to the side of the ball as he brings the ball backward. Ron Palombi, Jr., slightly wraps the ball behind his back during his delivery. All four of these gentlemen are outstanding players who have won dozens of tournaments among them.

Despite their accomplishments, it is far easier to bowl well with an armswing that's by the book. Their ability to achieve an exact duplication of movements shot after shot has been maximized by the great amount of bowling that they do. For the 99.9 percent of amateur players who don't roll hundreds of games per week, you will probably enjoy far more luck if you keep your movements as basic as possible.

For romantic results, try bowling's KISS system. KISS stands for *Keep It Straight and Simple.*

Your hand and wrist should be in a comfortable position. For right-handed players the ball should swing with the thumb around 2 o'clock with the fingers at 5 and 6

*Amleto Monacelli has employed a somewhat unorthodox style to become a PBA superstar.* Russ Vitale

o'clock. Left-handed bowlers should have your thumb at 10 o'clock with your fingers at 6 and 7 o'clock.

Once again, there are no rules to which you must conform. All-time great Marshall Holman, the PBA's 1987 Player of the Year, uses a closed hand position in which his thumb is found around the noon position. Two-time Player of the Year Monacelli wraps his hand around his ball. It's in an open position in which his palm faces outward during the top of his backswing. His fingers are around 4 o'clock during his release.

Some of the Tour's straight players stay behind the ball. Incidentally, a straight player isn't necessarily one who drinks milk and goes to bed before the news. That term refers to guys who prefer to impart a minimal amount of hook on most lane conditions. PBA standouts Tony Westlake, Dave Ferraro, Ernie Schlegel, and Don Genalo are masters at keeping their palms behind the ball during their deliveries.

The other extreme is represented by "Hookin' " Bob Handley. Known for his huge hook, Bob places his thumb at 3 o'clock.

As for me, I'm usually in the 3:30 to 4:30 range. As I come through the bottom of my swing my fingers rotate in a counterclockwise motion covering about two "hours" of the clock (e.g., from 5 to 3 o'clock). Virtually all of the top pros are versatile enough to adjust hand positions to combat different lane conditions.

Most players are best advised to find a position that feels comfortable and works well for you. Regardless of which you pick, be careful to avoid "topping the ball," a bad habit that hurts many amateurs. Do not allow your thumb to get in front of or on top of the ball during the delivery of your strike shot. Be sure to lock your wrist into the same position throughout the entire armswing.

Your wrist can be placed into one of the three basic positions: flat, cocked, or bent backward. A cocked wrist will increase the amount your shot will hook, assuming

**The three basic wrist positions. From the right they are: cocked, flat, and backward.** Dan Chidester

that you don't incorrectly release the ball on the upswing. More on that later.

Bending your wrist backward will "kill" the hook. That's a good strategy on those occasions when you are looking to maximize accuracy, such as when you are attempting to cover a single-pin spare. The flat wrist will give you a moderate amount of hook. No matter which option you choose, make certain that your wrist position does not deviate during any segment of your delivery.

There's another option, but it's for pros and very advanced amateurs only. It's known as *loading and unloading* or *wristing*. The player's hand is cupped during the downswing. During the release the wrist returns to the normal (flat) position. The hand is still cupped as the thumb exits but is flat by the time the fingers have departed. The result is that the fingers impart more ball rotation for great pin-carrying power. Among the pros who use this technique to great effect are Kelly Coffman, Wayne Webb, and Bob Benoit. I have also used it to my advantage on occasion.

**The Pushaway** Just prior to starting your motion you may wish to take a deep breath to help relax your body. It is important that you don't take too long in the address position, because muscles that are locked into the same position for any appreciable length of time will become tight. Good bowling requires a state of relaxation.

As the name implies, you push the ball away from your body. This occurs as you take your first major step (the initial stride for four-step players or the second step for you five-steppers). The pushaway's start coincides with your heel leaving the floor.

I like to lift the ball slightly upward and then move it forward as if I were handing it to an imaginary person standing in front of me. The key is to allow the ball to descend on its own, propelled by gravity and not by your arm muscles.

**In Dave's ideal pushaway he hands the ball forward to avoid "instant death."**
Dan Chidester

A proper pushaway is smooth and even. It should never be erratic or involve a jerking motion. Noted bowling coach John Jowdy refers to a bad pushaway as "instant death." He's right, for what starts out wrong is almost certain to end up wrong.

Some players prefer their bowling arm to be straight at this point. I feel more comfortable with a slight bend of the elbow. Either way, your ability to execute a good pushaway will play an enormous role in the outcome of your shot.

For me, locking the arm can cause problems. Doing so tends to make the shoulder that's attached to my bowling arm move inward. It gets closer to the foul line than my nonbowling shoulder. I find that the ball will invariably return to the position upon my release, even if I've opened up my shoulder during the height of my backswing. The result is a shot that goes left of my target.

My elbow will naturally straighten during the ball's descent. I see no need (nor any benefit) to locking my arm prior to that point.

Think of your arm as a pendulum. Imagine a piece of

string that has a heavy object (like a bowling ball) attached to one end. Picture that string held aloft and swinging freely. That, in essence, is how your armswing should work. To do that right requires a proper pushaway with the inside of the ball in a position that will allow it to swing just wide of your hip during both the backswing and the downswing.

You want to push the ball along the line that you intend it to take during your swing. There are some minor adjustments that we pros use. Remember, these are advanced techniques—not to be attempted until the fundamentals of a good pushaway have been mastered.

A bowling lane promotes a big hook when it's extremely dry. When little oil is present, I play a deep inside line. That means that I'm on the far left side of the approach and will aim the ball to the right. To accommodate that angle, I must turn my body toward my target. In that case, I will push the ball slightly to the right. I find that helps me maintain accuracy. It should be noted that many coaches prefer to see players always square with a straight pushaway.

My strategy has the ball come slightly behind my body during the backswing. That makes it easier for my hand to come around the ball to impart a harder hit on my release for greater hook and carrying power.

Conversely, when I'm pointing up my shots as I stand far to the right side of the lane, I push the ball slightly to my left. My subsequent armswing is slightly right-to-left, which, once again, helps me to hit my target.

Another minor adjustment—one that you can try after you've achieved an appreciable level of proficiency—involves ball speed. To obtain more velocity, just hold the ball higher during your address position, or hand it farther upward during your pushaway. To decrease your ball speed, hold it lower or hand it out at a lower height, or do both.

Another option—the one that works best for me—is to increase or decrease my foot speed. I push the ball away a little faster with my feet moving slightly quicker to compensate. After years of practice, my armswing naturally conforms to what my feet are doing. Once again, the millions of games I've bowled make that a feasible strategy for me to use. All of that practice has given me natural timing. Use trial and error to decide if you do better by changing the height at which you hold the ball and push it away or are more successful by altering your foot speed.

**The Armswing** It's been said that the golfer's prayer goes something like this: "Lord, please give me the strength to swing easy." Bowlers have a similar refrain. Remember, it's vital that our armswing should be a natural movement, much like that pendulum in which the object

**The pendulum armswing leads to a straight follow-through that's aimed at the target.** Dan Chidester

swings freely from the string. If the armswing is executed correctly, the bowling ball does all of the work and your arm muscles are just along for the ride.

One of the most difficult aspects of bowling is to disengage your arm muscles. The object is for the bowling ball to swing your arm and *not* the other way around. Believe me, this is a far more difficult proposition than it sounds. The key is to think of that round black object as a wrecking ball with your arm as the wire.

As best you can, allow the ball to swing your arm. If you can do this following a straight pushaway, your armswing should be perfect. The height of your backswing will be determined by the weight of the ball and the height of your pushaway. In most cases, it will be about shoulder high.

Is it possible to fully disengage your muscles? I doubt it. You do need to use your muscles somewhat to release the shot at the bottom of your swing. But the freer the swing is of outside interference, the better off you will be. An obtainable goal is to aim for 70–75 percent freedom with but 25–30 percent control.

Your body should remain square to your target throughout your delivery. Once again, this is a rule that many pros seem to believe was made to be broken. Attend a PBA or LPBT event and you're sure to find several power players who open their bowling shoulder before coming square on their release.

Keep in mind just how many games these athletes roll in a given week. Even with that, they sometimes suffer from sub-par shot because their shoulder is either squared up prematurely or doesn't do so until after the shot was released.

In your case, I strongly recommend that all of your motions fall into these two categories: either parallel or perpendicular to your target at all times. Your body is square, your armswing is straight. The simplicity of your motions will help you to become more far consistent. Plus, square shoulders help in executing a straight armswing that is performed without any interference from your muscles.

As you improve, you may wish to adjust your ball speed to accommodate lane conditions. The nonmuscled armswing makes this alteration easier to execute. Remember that the key to a straight armswing unencumbered by the use of your muscles is to do everything right at the start. The ideal armswing always begins with a good pushaway.

**Footwork and Timing** Being *in time* refers to the principle that the release of your shot should coincide with the conclusion of your slide. Some players have *early* or *late* timing in which the ball is released either before their slide concludes or well after that foot has been planted. Any of these three options can work, but the key is always to be consistent in that relationship between slide and release.

Coordinating the series of movements between your armswing and your feet is far from easy. After a long layoff, even experienced players often find that their timing is the first quality that suffers.

Achieving consistent timing is essential to obtaining maximum leverage at the foul line, which results in better striking power. It is even more vital to those of you who don't have a straight armswing. If your arm moves in a circuitous motion (as shown in the accompanying diagram), a late or early release will send the ball to one side or the other. That's another reason that a straight armswing is such a plus: your ability to be accurate will not be compromised even on shots in which your timing is slightly off the mark.

There are two primary approaches you can select: the four-step delivery or the five-step delivery. Most players, including the great majority of top pros, take that extra stride. It's the easier of the two for maintaining a natural rhythm and flow. It also allows you to generate more ball speed without having to muscle your armswing.

The four-step is used by Brian Voss and Mark Williams,

*Circuitous
Armswing >*

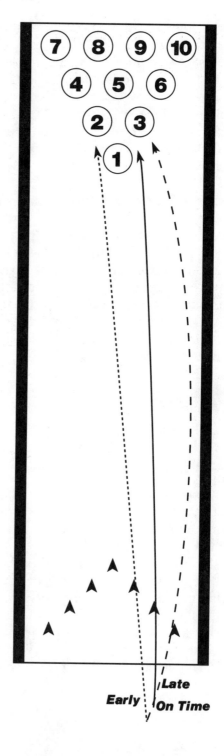

***1988 Player of the Year Brian Voss is among the PBA standouts who prefer the four-step delivery.*** Courtesy of Brunswick Corporation

who formerly used the five. It allows you to be more consistent with your timing.

To have good timing requires synchronizing your armswing with your footwork. So significant are your timing and your footwork that they merit separate discussion. Without mastering those items you cannot realize your potential. Therefore, we will explore that significant relationship between your armswing and your footwork in greater detail in the next chapter.

**The Release** It's often said that a player does a good job on his or her release by coming through the shot. Your ability to impart "lift" is what makes the difference between a ball that explodes through the rack and one that weakly deflects after hitting the pocket.

As you near the bottom of your swing your thumb will exit from the ball. Your middle and ring fingers will be rotating in a counterclockwise direction (clockwise for you left-handed players). Coach Jowdy refers to this as the *half-turn*.

Some power players use a bigger turning motion to impart a bigger hook at the back end of the lane. Monacelli, Miller, Ballard, Holman, and Coffman come to mind. Others cut down on their hook by keeping their hand behind the ball. More on that later.

For those who do rotate, the hand/finger turn begins

*The thumb exits the ball first to allow the fingers to impart a powerful roll.* Dan Chidester

as the ball nears the bottom of the downswing. My bowling hand is approximately one foot behind an imaginary perpendicular plane drawn from my sliding foot.

It's important not to over-turn. If my fingers go past the 3 o'clock position (9 o'clock for southpaws) I'm susceptible to topping the ball. I'm likely to miss my target to the left with the ball spinning like a top instead of gripping the lane.

Even if I should get lucky enough to hit the pocket, it is unlikely that my shot will have sufficient power to succeed. Because there is less ball surface in contact with the lane, less inertia is generated. More often than not, this lack of gripping power will cause the shot to deflect upon impact. That leads to a variety of splits.

I can only think of one pro who has done well with a shot that spins. Since becoming a full-time Tour pro in 1977, Tom Baker has won seven national PBA Tour events. He spins the ball because he has to, however, not because that's his preference. A serious wrist injury several years back made Tom alter his release. Due to the way his ball rolls, he's been nicknamed "the Helicopter" by his fellow pros. Although Tom is a gifted and fundamentally sound player, his spin shot makes it extremely difficult for him to be competitive on heavy oil conditions.

The only time having a spin is a plus is on extremely dry lanes (which tend to hook a lot). Having a spin without topping the ball will cause it to roll well down the lane before it begins to curve toward the pocket. Some pros have demonstrated an amazing ability to spin a ball on dry lanes with adequate power. Among these are Joe Berardi, Ted Hannahs, Butch Soper, and Baker.

You want to release the ball just as your hand passes in front of that imaginary perpendicular plane from your sliding foot. Project it outward—not upward—onto the lane. The next time that you watch a PBA telecast, notice how the pros do not drop the ball during their downswing. In the modern game, they no longer loft it, either. Some use what is now known as soft loft. More on that later.

***LPBT standout Jeanne
Maiden follows
through at her target.***
Courtesy Ladies Pro Bowlers
Tour

Once again, not all of us are perfect examples. Hall of
Fame member Larry Laub broke the rules by dropping the
ball at the bottom of his downswing. While I don't wish in
any way to demean the accomplishments of a previous
generation of stars, I suspect that Larry's technique would
not fare nearly so well on modern lane conditions in which
pin-crushing power is a virtual prerequisite for Tour sur-
vival.

Having noticed how we pros release our shots, you
should then observe lower-average players. You'll quickly
realize how many of them either drop the ball into the lane
or heave it through the air.

Do not let your shoulders slump well in front of your
body. To maximize leverage, your shoulders should lean
approximately 10 degrees forward so that they are square.

***Former Team USA star Kim Terrell keeps her nonsliding (left) foot in contact with the lane during and after her release to help her stay down with her shot.***
Courtesy Ladies Pro Bowlers Tour

The shoulders should be on the same plane that is directly above the ankle of your sliding foot at the point of release.

A natural and slight bend from the waist is ideal to avoid throwing the ball into the lane. Most of the bending should be from the knee of your sliding foot.

Stroke through the ball as you release your shot. From the start of the downswing (which follows your pushaway) until after the shot is released, your bowling arm should be straight. A bent elbow makes for a muscled swing.

Extend your follow-through toward your desired target. One danger to avoid is rearing up at the foul line. Stay down with your shot at least until after it has crossed the arrows.

Bowlers who pull up violently upon releasing the ball will lose their shot off their hand. A significant loss of power will result. A good method for avoiding rearing up is to concentrate on eyeing your target arrow until well after your shot's motions have been concluded. Remind yourself to watch your ball as it crosses through the arrows. Doing so will bring you the added benefit of knowing if you've hit your target.

Your eyes are a key ingredient in being accurate. Your arm has a tendancy to go in the direction you're looking. If you don't believe me, try the following exercise. Concentrate on an object in the room. Next, point at it. Your finger will automatically point exactly where you were looking. It's the same in bowling.

Keeping your eyes riveted on your target throughout your entire delivery will help keep your head steady. If you wish to discover the importance of your eyes, try another experiment. The next time you bowl, close your eyes at the

*Three-time Tournament of Champions winner Mike Durbin used an unusual technique for handling pressure situations.* Courtesy Professional Bowlers Association

start of your slide. I'll bet you my favorite bass fishing pole that the ball will go far to the right of your target.

In fact, I know of one great pro who told me that he actually used that principle to his advantage. All of us react differently to pressure situations. Many bowlers tend to grip the ball too tightly (Touring pros call it *squeezing a shot*) and try to fit it into the pocket instead of enjoying a smooth and natural swing.

To combat that tendency, when under great pressure, Hall of Fame player Mike Durbin would intentionally close his eyes just prior to executing the release. That helped him to give his shot plenty of room.

Keeping those eyes on your target until the ball has at least reached the arrows yields another dividend. Should your shot miss the pocket, it will allow you to determine if it was due to your inaccuracy or whether the lane's oil pattern has changed (thus causing the alley to make your ball hook more or less). Only with that knowledge can you decide whether to make an adjustment in how you are playing the lane.

If this sounds complicated, don't fret. I promise that in Chapter 4 I will teach you all you need to know about making adjustments.

**The Follow-Through** The appearance you give after releasing the ball is strictly a matter of personal preference. As with all aspects of the game, being consistent counts for a lot.

Some pros *post*. That is, they seem to exaggerate their follow-through by holding it for a considerable period of time. It's almost as if they were posing for a bowling statue. Included in that category are Durbin, George Pappas, and Patty Ann.

Others, like myself, allow our arm to drop to our side as soon as it's done its job. The reason that isn't to my detriment is because it occurs only after I've come through the ball to execute a proper release.

Your follow-through can provide certain clues as to

what has preceded it. The orthodox player has his or her hand come through toward the target. If your hand ends up on anything other than a direct plane from your release to your target you might not be executing a straight and unmuscled armswing. Should that be the case, a bit of work on improving your pushaway could be in order.

## A FEW FINAL WORDS ON YOUR DELIVERY

In a sport in which the only criterion for success is how many, it's easy to fall into a style that has more movements than a Swiss watch. That's even truer than ever before given the large number of role models on the pro circuits whose styles are extremely unorthodox.

Of course there is no one right way to bowl. But for those of you who don't have the time or inclination to bowl upward of five times a week like I do, you will probably find that you are far better served by a style that is in harmony with the traditional approach to the game.

By adopting a conventional (i.e., stroker's) style you will not only improve, you should also become far more consistent. An added bonus is that the simplicity of your movements means that it should take you far less time to warm up prior to competing. That ability to reach peak efficiency rapidly will become very much appreciated as you improve. While others are still "getting the kinks out," you can experiment with different strike lines and bowling ball types, and work on reading the lane. All of these things will become important factors toward your success as you become a good player.

Your challenge is to become as fundamentally sound as soon as possible. I'm convinced that a simple style that's by the book will show itself to be an even greater asset as you improve. Never forget my "Honeymooners Theory"—real bowlers are like Ralph and Alice Kramden. No matter how bad things get, always be ready to KISS and make up.

With that in mind, let's review the bowling traits that come highly recommended. To KISS, you should have a

***Nikki Gianulias's by-the-book style includes the recommended steady head throughout her delivery.*** Courtesy Ladies Pro Bowlers Tour

straight armswing in which the ball propels your arm, square shoulders throughout your delivery, an ability to keep your eyes riveted on your target at all times, good and consistent timing, and a locked wrist during at least the majority of your delivery process. End it with a comfortable follow-through.

# 2
# Footwork and Timing

It has been said that in life, timing is everything. So too with bowling. With the possible exception of the circuitous armswing, poor timing is the most common flaw among middle- and lower-average players.

By timing, I'm referring to the relationship between your footwork and your armswing. While helpful, it's not essential that they be synchronized. It *is* imperative that you obtain a degree of consistency in that relationship between the end of your slide and the release of your shot. That's one quality that all of the top pros possess.

Inconsistent timing causes a variety of problems. Not the least of these is a lack of leverage at the point of release, which will deprive your ball of pin-carrying power. If it seems that you get "robbed" far too often, the chances are that the cause of this seeming injustice is not prejudicial pins. I suspect that pieces of wood lack an ability to pick on you. While luck can play a role in a specific shot's outcome, those who seem to be unfortunate over long periods of time are probably not executing first-rate shots.

Bad timing, especially when combined with an armswing that's not straight, results in inaccuracy. It also

***Jackie Sellers
synchronizes the
release of her shot
with the conclusion
of her slide.*** Courtesy
Ladies Pro Bowlers Tour

makes it harder for you to achieve a level of consistency in your performance.

To review: *late* timing occurs when your slide concludes prior to the release of your shot. Conversely, *early* timing refers to the handful of players who release the ball before concluding their slide. And being *in time* means that the slide ends as the ball is being released.

The bottom line is that there are great bowlers who have late timing. There are great bowlers who have the traditional approach of being in time. There have even been a few good ones who have early timing (although it doesn't come with my recommendation).

Regardless of which of these three options best suits your needs, it's important that your timing be consistent. To be late one shot and early the next is an all-too-common flaw.

Many power players opt to be intentionally late. They feel that they gain leverage by planting first. Strokers tend to be in time. Being early is rare among better players, but it is possible to enjoy success that way as well.

As with many items we discussed in the previous chapter, I recommend that the occasional bowler select the traditional style, assuming that you feel comfortable doing so. Being in time is far easier to duplicate shot after shot than being late or early. However, given the greater emphasis on rolling strikes in the modern game, you may find that being slightly late works to your advantage. Either way, achieving a level of consistency with your timing is extremely important.

Another matter involving personal preference involves the number of strides that you take. In both the amateur and professional ranks, the five-step delivery is the most prevalent. It features a short initial step to begin your

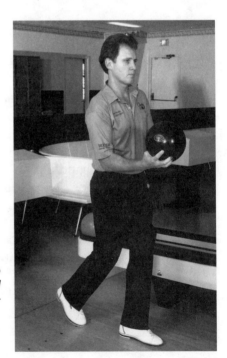

*A five-step player, David puts the ball into motion on his second stride.* Dan Chidester

movements toward the foul line. The pushaway is executed on your second step.

In addition to the aforementioned Voss and Mark Williams, top star Mike Aulby is in the four-step contingent. They all feel that this option makes consistent timing easier to obtain.

I like the added fifth step because I find it maintains a natural rhythm and flow in my movements. The five-step style makes it easier for me to generate greater ball speed when conditions or a certain spare-conversion strategy calls for playing a more direct line.

A handful of pros have used more or fewer steps. Del Warren spent many years with a three-step style, while all-time greats Mark Roth and Monacelli have been known to take as many as seven strides. Given how unusual those are, we will concentrate on the two options that I suspect are employed by at least 95 percent of pros and amateurs alike.

## THE FIRST STEP(S)

What starts out right is likely to conclude correctly. What starts wrong will almost assuredly end wrong. Given that premise, the importance of coordinating your pushaway with the first phases of your footwork can't be sufficiently emphasized.

As a member of the five-step contingent, I do not put the bowling ball into motion until my second step. That first step is at most a half-stride. Some players, such as Mark Baker, merely shuffle their foot a few inches forward without the bottom of the shoe leaving the lane.

That movement is made with the foot opposite your bowling hand. As a right-handed player, I move my left foot. A lefty who selects a five-step delivery begins with his or her right foot.

Either way, lean your body slightly forward. That modest tilt—which is at most 10 degrees—helps generate a natural momentum toward the foul line. You wish to be upright and stiff no more than you want to lean too far forward. Doing the latter would take your center of gravity forward of your feet, resulting in decreased stability at the point of release.

## THE KEY STEP

Award-winning bowling instructional columnist Tom Kouros likes to refer to what he calls "the key step." By that he means the first step of a four-step delivery (the second step for those who use the five-step style).

Either way, your key step involves the leg that's on the same side as your bowling hand. As my heel leaves the ground I start my pushaway. I push the ball slightly upward. Others like to hand it forward on a straight plane. Either of these options is OK.

Do *not*, however, allow the ball to be pushed (or dropped) downward. Dropping the ball isn't inherently a fatal flaw, although it does prove detrimental to most players. It can be overcome if combined with a subsequent corrective maneuver.

**Dave's straight
pushaway coincides
with his second step.**
Dan Chidester

After dropping the ball, you must execute a compensatory step to avoid early timing. To do so adds two more components to your delivery. The more movements you must execute, the more things that can go wrong. That's especially true for those of you who bowl but once or twice a week. Perhaps that's why very few top-level players lack a good pushaway.

Moreover, dropping the ball means that you must engage your arm muscles. Remember that the ideal pushaway ends when gravity takes over. That approach allows for a pendulum armswing that has the desired degree of freedom for good shot making.

As your heel hits the lane, the ball has reached its full extension. Your next step will begin as the ball begins its natural descent.

I highly recommend heel-to-toe footwork on the key step and for five-step players who opt for anything beyond a short shuffle step to start their footwork.

The key step is not quite a full stride. The traditional style called for each succeeding step to be longer than the one that preceded it. The logic behind that is to allow for a slow building of momentum while enjoying an even increase in tempo.

As we will soon see, many bowlers who don't use a conventional address position and/or pushaway shun this strategy. They use what is known as a corrective step to bring themselves back into time. For the rest of us, the slow lengthening of subsequent strides is a plus.

## THE SECOND (THIRD) STEP

Your key step and pushaway having concluded, it's now time to step forward with the leg that's opposite from your bowling hand. This stride is slightly longer than your key step was. As the foot meets the lane the ball is well into the backswing. At this point the ball should be approximately six inches to one foot behind your body.

Keep in mind that the proper pushaway has allowed the ball to swing freely. By stepping directly forward on all

*Featuring a good knee bend, perfect timing, and ideal balance and riveting his eyes on his target during his timing step have prepared junior bowler Larry Antinozzi to make a good shot.* Dan Chidester

of your strides, you allow for the armswing to remain largely unencumbered by the unnecessary use of your arm muscles.

## THE TIMING STEP

In most cases, the third (fourth) stride sees the ball reach the apex of the backswing. For most of us, that means it is at shoulder height.

Some shorter bowlers prefer to use higher backswings in an effort to generate greater ball speed. Among those who have enjoyed considerable success doing so are Peter Weber, Monacelli, and Chris Warren.

Conversely, many taller bowlers bring the ball only slightly above waist height. It's their feeling that doing so allows for more control.

As with many generalizations, there are exceptions to the exceptions. Steve Cook is a 14-time champion who became the 13th man in PBA history to top $750,000 in career earnings. At 6'7", Steve towers over Warren (5'5"), Weber (5'7"), and Monacelli (5'8"). Unlike most taller players, Steve has a backswing that's so high that he has, at times, actually hit the overhead score screens with his ball.

Despite their dramatic differences in build, Cook and Warren look similar at this point of their deliveries. That their bowling ball is at the top of the swing as the next-to-last step ends speaks to why they both enjoy consistently outstanding timing.

Other players use this stride as their corrective step. Holman is in the PBA Hall of Fame and Webb is a sure bet to join him upon becoming eligible following his 35th birthday. Wayne is short (5'5") while Marshall is of average (5'9") height.

Both like to hold the ball very low during their address. Marshall starts with the ball supported by both hands in front of him while Wayne dangles it on his side. Wayne lifts his left toe upward before the ball moves forward and upward. Marshall puts the ball into the swing far earlier than the norm, while Wayne's starting position means that his hand is ahead of his footwork during the early portions of his delivery.

The last thing that either player wants is for his release to precede his sliding foot to the foul line. Should that occur the ball would be lifted and misdirected upon its release.

Both stars avoid this by taking a far shorter stride on their next-to-last step. Not everybody waits that long to make a correction. Roth's second step tends to be shorter. Steve Wunderlich, who is the consummate stylist, shortens his third step.

Given that I use a more orthodox starting position

Courtesy Ladies Pro Bowlers Tour

Russ Vitale

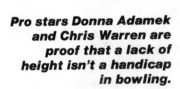

*Pro stars Donna Adamek and Chris Warren are proof that a lack of height isn't a handicap in bowling.*

than does Wayne or Marshall, my fourth step is longer than my third but shorter than my subsequent slide. I use it to help generate leg power by pushing off my toes at this juncture. For that reason, some people even refer to this as the power step.

## THE SLIDE

By tradition, the final aspect of footwork is the slide. It is the longest of the steps and involves a deep knee bend. The execution of a good slide coupled with other important fundamentals allows you to obtain maximum leverage at the point of release. Coupled with being balanced, this helps to give you a powerful strike shot.

As with other aspects of bowling, not all of today's pros go by the book. There is a contingent who plant their foot and then hit their release. Examples include the winners of three of bowling's most prestigious four events of 1990: Ferraro (Firestone Tournament of Champions), Chris Warren (American Bowling Congress Masters), and

***The slide.*** Dan Chidester

**Dave's outstanding technique and leverage allow his legs to be exploited to their fullest in this sequence of photos.** Dan Chidester

Ron Palombi, Jr. (Seagram's Coolers United States Open). Except for Dave, the players who do so tend to be twisters and power players.

In fact, Warren used sneakers during the 1991 Celebrity Denver Open. His logic was that the approaches were slippery and he wished to enjoy maximum traction. Had I tried the same, I probably would just be landing now.

In contrast, Holman slides several feet before releasing his shot. Most of the rest of us slide a couple of feet.

I like to point my sliding foot in the direction of the target. That follows the stroker's philosophy of all movements being parallel or perpendicular.

Some big-hook bowlers turn their sliding foot inward. By doing that, they point their toes toward the gutter that's on the same side as their bowling hand. Handley actually turns his foot sideways as he finishes his delivery. So dramatic is that pivot that I once saw him foul because the *heel* of his sliding foot crossed over the line!

Many players like to slide with their toes pointed slightly inward. I have heard of one prominent pro who suffered through a prolonged slump that was caused in large part by his foot pointing away from his bowling hand. That may sound like a minor and trivial flaw. Believe me, it may be minor but it's not trivial. With so many top-flight competitors on the PBA Tour, the slightest loss of leverage can result in failing to carry one shot every other game. By week's end, hundreds of pins have been lost.

I'm constantly amazed at how the smallest of details can upset the bowler's applecart. No wonder some of us spend so many hours in front of our television sets studying tapes of how we have performed on the lanes that day.

## THE LEVERAGE WINDOW

In bowling parlance, your release should occur while you are in the leverage window. As throughout the delivery, your shoulders remain slightly forward of the waist. They are on the same plane as your sliding foot (slightly behind the knee). The knee of the sliding foot is bent to help augment your leverage.

The thumb will naturally begin to exit from its hole when the ball is about one foot behind the sliding foot. It should be released like an airplane lands. The ball gradually descends and then levels out so it's on more of an even plane as it is released. You want to neither drop it onto the lane nor throw it upward.

Upon releasing the ball, your arm is straight. As a matter of personal preference, I extend my nonbowling (left) arm outward to aid my balance. That balancing motion helps to counteract the up to 16 pounds that's in my other hand.

## IN CONCLUSION

Consistent timing is one of bowling's essentials. No matter how unorthodox a player might appear to the naked eye, all top pros have achieved a great level of proficiency in this basic skill.

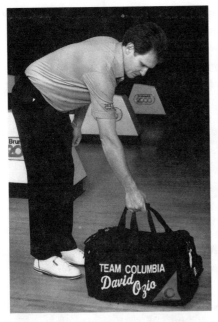

*The leverage principle: lifting a heavy object in front of your body engages only your back muscles, risking an injury. Having that object at your side allows for leg strength to be employed. So, too, with the release of your shot.* Dan Chidester

I won't suggest that it's impossible for you to better yourself without first acquiring consistent timing. But to do so would at the very least be extremely difficult.

If the relationship between your slide (or plant) and shot release varies, so will the amount of hit that you impart on the ball. As such, some shots will hook more while others will hook less. Your ability to carry a pocket hit—indeed, the very accuracy required to reach the pocket—will be compromised.

Timing is the one skill that you can practice without having to visit a bowling center. You can do it on a linoleum floor with a tennis ball in your bowling hand. While that's not as good as the real thing, it's preferable to doing nothing during those long stretches between trips to the lanes.

The next time you're watching pros bowl, observe how consistent their footwork and timing have become. Mastering both is one of the keys toward enjoying a great improvement in your game.

# 3
# Bowling Equipment

Having the proper equipment and the right bowling ball that fits correctly is vital. I could no more compete successfully on the Professional Bowlers Association Tour with second-rate equipment than Picasso could have produced a masterpiece using finger paint.

In the history of bowling there has never been a wider range of equipment available than there is today. Making educated decisions on how you spend your dollars will permit you to knock over the most pins that your talents will allow.

Once you have decided that you like to bowl—and I assume anyone who has already gone to the trouble of buying an instructional book is well beyond that stage—you should own your own bowling ball, bag, and shoes.

Yes, you can rent the latter, and all centers have balls available for use. But the shoes you rent are ambidextrous. They are designed to be used by either a left- or a right-handed player. Custom shoes have different surfaces on the bottom of the right shoe and left shoe to help your footwork. More on that in a moment.

**The well-stocked pro shop such as this one at Beacon's (NY) Southern Dutchess Bowl can help you with all of your equipment needs.** Dan Chidester

As for bowling balls, having the proper weight and fit is essential. It's almost impossible to find an alley ball that meets either of those criteria, much less both. Trying to bowl with a ball that is too light or too heavy or doesn't fit your hand makes about as much sense as going for a jog while wearing a suit, tie, and dress shoes.

## BOWLING SHOES

How much must one spend to obtain the basic needed equipment? Shoes range from $20 up to approximately $125. A pro or a top-level amateur player who rolls hundreds of games a week needs the added support that the most expensive pairs feature.

As for the majority of players, there is little justification for spending more than $35 to $60. Within that range you can buy a pair that should last for several seasons. Unless you plan on entering tournaments in which you may bowl a great number of games in one day, you will find plenty of comfort and style in the middle price range models.

As I mentioned, there are left- and right-handed shoes. The bottom of the sliding foot (which is on the opposite side from your bowling hand) is designed to minimize the amount of friction encountered between you and the lane. This promotes a smooth slide that will help you release the ball to the best of your ability.

The other shoe is made for traction to help grip the lane. As you improve, you will find that this aids the amount of power generated by your ball by allowing your legs to contribute to the leverage you obtain at the point of release.

For the right-handed player, the right shoe has a stopper sole made of rubber with a leather toe for maximum wear. The other shoe is made of a softer leather to promote your slide.

Different shoe models have different characteristics.

*The bottoms of the three custom shoes on the left are for the sliding foot. The corresponding shoes for the opposite foot (right) help to augment traction on varying types of approach surfaces.* Dan Chidester

Most pros carry a few pairs so they are prepared in case they should bowl in a center whose approaches are unusually slippery or sticky. It's unlikely that the place in which you compete would fall into either of those two unusual extremes.

Nevertheless, you should be certain that is the case before purchasing your shoes. That's because there are models available specifically designed to combat extraordinary lane conditions.

Although you can buy loafer-style shoes, I recommend ones that tie. The added support will be appreciated on those occasions when you must bowl after spending most of that day on your feet.

## BOWLING BALLS

A lot of beginners grab a house ball. Most of them are afraid of the ball hanging on their hand, so they select one that is too light and in which an elephant could just about fit its paw into the thumbhole.

There is a common misconception that a lighter ball with big holes allows one to gain control. In fact, the exact opposite is the case. The tendency to fling a lighter ball is a lot worse than a ball that's slightly too heavy for your level of strength. In that case, you will be forced to be a bit smoother in your delivery, which is far more conducive to being accurate.

However, a ball that is significantly too heavy is just as detrimental as one that's too light. Its movement during your armswing could cause you to lose balance. You don't want the ball to swing you, you want to be able to swing the ball.

Another problem is that you will bowl with a different ball almost every week. You can't possibly develop a consistent delivery when the very weight and fit of your ball keeps changing. One week you will be able to put your thumb in all the way and another time only halfway. The point at which you actually release your shot will differ.

If you must use an alley ball, then you should know

how to select one that is right for you (or, to be more truthful, you'll be lucky to find a ball that is the least worst for your needs). The most important factors are having the correct length of span and the proper size thumbhole.

The span is the distance between the thumb and finger holes. Insert your thumb fully into the ball and lay your fingers flat across the other holes. Stretch your hand slightly. The bottom of the finger holes (the part of the holes closest to the thumbhole) should correspond with the first knuckle of your fingers.

Only with a proper span will your thumb exit the ball at the right time. Ideally, the thumb releases at the bottom of your downswing. The fingers remain in the ball slightly longer, supplying lift and rotation.

Do not mistake lift for loft. Lift is how you release your shot so that it impacts powerfully against the pins. Loft is the act by which you launch your ball upward so that it bounces onto the lane. Whereas loft was once considered part of a pro's standard arsenal, it is hardly used now on

*If you don't own your own ball, take care to select the alley ball that best fits your needs.* Dan Chidester

modern lane conditions. In most cases, lofting produces what we pros call a dead roll. By the time your ball has reached the pins, much of its energy has been expended, making it inefficient.

Late exit can cause you to inadvertently loft your shot. At the very least, you will be releasing your shot after your arm has passed through the leverage window. The power that should be transferred from your legs to the ball is lost.

A delayed exit can be caused by a span that is too long coupled with an improper pitch. Improper pitch? No, that's not what happens when Roger Clemens's curveball doesn't dip. Rather, it's the angle at which the hole is drilled into the ball.

That's one reason that the ball you meant to roll at the pins more closely resembles an infield fly rule pop-up. A short span forces your hand to squeeze the ball. That's not desirable if you are trying to knock over pins but it's great if you are a man trying to impress a woman on the next lane who loves big biceps.

Moreover, an inadequate span that has lessened the distance between your thumb and fingers makes for less ball rotation, which in turn means less hook. While that's not desirable at most levels of the sport, there are times that pros and highly advanced amateur players intentionally use it to their advantage.

Ultradry lanes make it desireable to roll the ball straighter. There are Touring pros who use conventional-grip balls for some spare shots and others who try shorter spans in that case. My good friend Steve Wunderlich is a prime example. However, Steve's strategy is one that I don't advise for the typical player.

Similarly, a thumbhole that is too big causes problems. You may find yourself dropping the ball onto the lane. Or to avoid doing that you may squeeze it so hard that you can't execute a smooth release. Squeezing is detrimental to shot making but it's great for developing blisters and helping to send your ball flying upward.

Both of the finger holes and the thumbhole should be snug but not tight. The best guideline is that one side of each finger and the thumb should be touching the side of the hole. Meanwhile, there is the slightest distance between each finger and the thumb and the opposite side of the hole. As you insert your hand into the ball you should not feel any snugness until you reach the second joint of the two fingers.

The odds are long for finding an alley ball with a proper fit. The holes on heavier balls are usually very large while those on light balls are extremely small. That often forces people to use a ball that fits their hand but is too heavy, because they can't wedge themselves into the one that is the right weight for their level of strength.

That's why I strongly recommend that you buy your own ball. If you are going to learn how to bowl the right way it is important that you start out right. Otherwise, poorly fitting equipment could cause you to develop bad habits. Bowling is tough enough to master without placing handicaps in your way.

Aside from the technical aspects, there is an even better reason not to experiment with alley balls. An ill-fitting ball, like that shoe I alluded to earlier, hurts. I've seen some nasty-looking blisters that resulted when players used equipment that didn't fit properly. If you want pain, take up boxing. If it's pleasure you desire from your leisure time, buy a ball that will fit your hand properly.

Assuming that I have convinced you to own your own ball, please also consider the importance of spending slightly more money for your purchase. Buy that ball at a pro shop.

## WHERE TO BUY

Think how great a $300 pair of shoes looks with the right suit. Now imagine purchasing the nicest pair on the rack only to discover that they are a size 8 and your feet are a size 10. I suspect the value of those shoes would plummet in direct proportion to the pain you'd soon be forced to withstand.

Likewise, a $130 urethane ball, which represents the best in state-of-the-art equipment, is of no use if it doesn't fit your hand properly. The most significant aspect of your purchase isn't what ball you buy or even how much you spend. Far more important is who fits and drills the ball. I would no sooner allow a typical sporting goods store sales-man to drill my ball than I would allow a dentist to drill my teeth without first applying anesthesia.

I consider myself to have a fair degree of expertise in this area. Even so, when I'm on the Tour I don't drill my own equipment. Instead, I and virtually all of my fellow pros pay a fee to the PBA Tour's Players Services Director Larry Lichstein simply because he's a master at ball drilling.

The price tags in a pro shop are higher than what you

*House pro Steve Ferraro provides Laurie with a custom fit. Paying the extra few dollars for the services of an expert ball driller is a smart investment.* Dan Chidester

will find across the street at a sporting goods store. Trust me, you will get what you pay for.

First of all, the better ball manufacturers only sell their top-of-the-line equipment in pro shops. The balls that they send to sporting goods stores are often seconds. The slight defects, which tend to be cosmetic in nature, pale in significance when compared to the problems caused by a poorly drilled ball.

The person who measures and then customizes your bowling ball should be an expert. The pro shop operator does that for his or her living. With rare exception, he or she has attended several seminars on ball drilling and is aware of the latest advances. The salesperson in the sporting goods store has a passing knowledge of everything from skis to soccer balls to batting helmets.

While you are almost certain *not* to get the level of service you deserve from a sporting goods store, you are not necessarily assured of the perfect fit from a pro shop. Most of these places do an outstanding job, but there are some that aren't up to par.

The more serious you are about your game—and the better you become—the more important it is to seek out the best ball driller in your area. Word of mouth is usually a good method. Chances are that the better bowlers in your region go to the best ball driller. If you don't know any top-level players, ask the person behind the desk when the most competitive league rolls. Attend a session and then seek out the better players afterward to discover where they spend their money.

On the other hand, you could save a few bucks by making that purchase at Joe's Wide World of Sports. Every January I more than pay my credit card bills from Lisa's Christmas shopping thanks to such folks. They come into my pro shop—the Winner's Edge at Crossroad Bowl in Beaumont—with the department store balls they received as gifts only to discover that the holes don't fit properly.

The most amazing ball was one with which the customer complained that he had trouble gaining a good grip.

Given that all of the holes were only one inch deep, it didn't take a Larry Lichstein to uncover his problem!

By the time guys like that have paid me to plug the old holes and put in a new set, they have spent a lot more money for a second-rate ball than if they had purchased a better-quality ball from me in the first place.

## THE THREE OPTIONS

Bowling balls come in three basic surface varieties: rubber, plastic, and urethane. In bowling's evolutionary scale, rubber balls replaced ones made of wood. They were most popular in the era of pinboys, which ended in the 1960s.

Rubber balls, although they last nearly forever, are virtually obsolete. They don't grip the lane with anywhere near the proficiency of either plastic or urethane. As such, the striking power produced by rubber isn't nearly as sub-

*Like all pros, LPBT star Robin Romeo relies almost exclusively on urethane bowling balls for her strike shots.*
Courtesy Ladies Pro Bowlers Tour

stantial as that of its rivals. To the best of my knowledge, only one of the major manufacturers still makes a rubber ball.

The difference between rubber and urethane is about the same as the difference between a baby's slap and Mike Tyson's left hook. One hits like a demolition ball, the other like a Ping-Pong ball.

Rubber's best quality is that it is probably the easiest to control. It's the least expensive. As such, it's a good ball with which beginners can learn to bowl.

Despite that, for all intents and purposes, your choice will probably be between a plastic or a urethane surface since rubber balls are becoming difficult to find.

Those watching PBA and LPBT events might think today's balls are made only of urethane. In the hands of accomplished players, urethane offers many big advantages. Without getting scientific, the basic urethane edge involves its ability to grip a lane, much like a radial tire hugs even a wet highway while cornering. That allows your shot to drive through the pins with a minimum of ball deflection. The result: more strikes, leading to higher scores.

Urethane is the latest in an evolutionary scale that began with wooden balls. It was 1973 when the bowling industry discovered just how significant an edge a player can gain from rolling superior equipment. It was at that time that Don McCune dominated the PBA Tour. Through trial and error, Don had discovered that soaking his ball in a special chemical substance softened the surface, allowing it to grip the lane more efficiently.

McCune won six titles that year. His $69,000 in earnings led the PBA. Had Don kept the secret of his success to himself, he might have dominated the Tour for years. Instead, he told others of his edge and the soaker ball was banned soon thereafter.

How important was the soaker ball to McCune? Except for 1973, Don never finished among the top 10 money winners in any other year, and he only won two tournaments in the rest of his career.

*Don McCune's discovery revolutionized bowling.*
Courtesy Professional Bowlers Association

It was that dramatic demonstration of the proverbial better mousetrap that led the major ball manufacturers to allocate small fortunes to research and development. The result was urethane.

There are several varieties of urethane balls on today's market. You can buy the same model with different characteristics. A Columbia 300 that has a dull (soft) surface will hook considerably more than the same model with a shiny (hard) surface. The advanced amateur player usually carries at least two balls with significantly different traits to be able to combat varying lane conditions.

Noted house pro Dave Heller has a saying that he can make a ball do anything with a quarter and a piece of sandpaper. What he means is that there are a number of ways to change a urethane ball's hooking pattern.

The quarter to which he refers is what it usually costs to polish a ball in a Lustre King Machine for two minutes. The wax added to the surface decreases friction and thus the amount the ball will hook.

Conversely, sandpaper or a similar abrasive material

can be used to roughen the ball's surface. This will add to the friction generated between the ball and the lane and increase how much it will hook.

Urethane's gripping action means that the ball will deflect less when hitting the pins. That makes for greater carrying power both on flush pocket hits and on light half-hits. It all adds up to greater scoring potential for the bowler who is advanced enough to impart proper hooking action and ball revolutions on his or her shots.

Urethane balls run the gamut from hard-shell (which hook very little for use on relatively dry lane surfaces) to porous (designed for oily lanes where it is more difficult to obtain enough hooking action). The quality of the top-of-the-line balls offered by the major manufacturers is outstanding and is getting better all of the time.

Expect to part with $110–$140 for the state-of-the-art urethane ball. However, there are also models made with a less expensive urethane that usually can be obtained at prices starting at about $65–$70. These hit harder than plastic without sacrificing much economy.

Another reason that a relative beginner should consider urethane is to avoid having to purchase another new ball when your skills become advanced enough to take advantage of the superior carrying power urethane features.

If money is no object, using the top-of-the-line ball certainly won't harm your game. It's just that you won't get the added benefits for which you have paid. If it is urethane you desire, start with one of the less expensive models.

Almost all lower-average players roll their shots end over end. When you have obtained a fair degree of accuracy, you will be ready for a fingertip grip, which will promote hooking action. At that point, I would suggest buying the better urethane ball.

Until then, plastic is just as efficient and it offers economy. Prices for a plastic ball usually start at around $50. Given that the advantages of urethane are virtually irrelevant for beginners, it seems silly to spend the extra money.

There are a few things that will probably occur after you first roll your new ball.

*1.* It will probably feel too tight. There are two reasons for this. Because you have most likely grown accustomed to squeezing an alley ball whose holes are far too large, you will find it strange to grip a ball that is actually the right size. This will feel more comfortable with time.

In addition, the smart ball driller always errs on the side of being too snug. A hole that isn't large enough can always be expanded, but once a hole is drilled too big, little can be done to correct it.

*2.* The thumbhole will be more generous than the other two. The size of your thumb varies in a number of ways. In high humidity it will tend to swell slightly. Every summer I actually have to open up the thumbholes on all of my bowling balls to compensate for a small increase in my thumb's size.

The more games you bowl, the more your hand will change. In most cases, the thumb will swell. With some people, including myself, it shrinks.

The thumbhole should be drilled to fit your thumb when it is at maximum size. At all other times that hole will be too large. You correct that by inserting a piece (or pieces) of special tape into the hole until the proper snug feel has been achieved. Ask your pro for pointers on how best to use tape.

*3.* You will probably request a ball weight that is too light for your needs. The alley ball that doesn't fit right will feel heavier because the grip isn't natural. The astute pro can usually tell what weight is most appropriate for your game. That judgment is based on observations of your size, strength, and with what degree of ease you are able to handle a certain weighted ball when it is handed to you.

## WHAT'S YOUR GRIP?

Another important reason to have an experienced ball driller is the knowledge of grips that person will possess. The three options are conventional, fingertip, and semifingertip.

A conventional grip is ideal for virtually all beginning and lower-average players. The fingers are fully inserted into the ball with the surface of the ball corresponding with the knuckles.

As the name implies, with a fingertip grip only the tips of the two fingers enter the ball (see photo on page 70). The semi-fingertip is drilled so that the fingers are inserted to a point between the knuckle and the first joint.

My general rule is that it's time to go to the fingertip grip when a male player has reached the 150–160-average plateau. There are exceptions. An athletic player who is

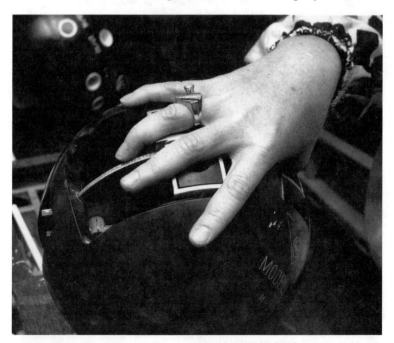

*A hand being fitted for a conventional grip ball in which the fingers will be inserted up to the player's knuckles.*
Dan Chidester

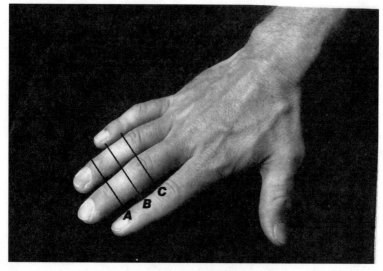

**3 Grips**    { A—*Fingertop Grip*
B—*Semifingertop Grip*
C—*Conventional Grip*

winging the ball at the pins isn't ready to make the change. A bowler who relies on being very accurate but can't carry many pocket hits might be a candidate to make the switch prior to reaching the 150 level.

With female players, I tend to be cautious in recommending such a change. I've seen a lot of women hurt their games by switching to a fingertip grip. If they aren't strong enough, especially with wrist power, it can be counterproductive.

I'm even more reluctant to drill a semifingertip grip. With the other two options you can pinpoint exactly how far to put your digits into the holes. Not so with the semifingertip. Having to estimate how far to place your fingers into the ball can result in being off by one-quarter of an inch. That hardly seems like much, but it can make a big difference when you exit from the ball during your release. Little errors at the foul line can result in one big mistake by the time your shot has reached the pins.

## IS THIN IN OR IS IT OK TO BE OVERWEIGHT?

What ball weight is right for you? Get the heaviest one you can handle without feeling uncomfortable or unnatural. You should be able to pick the ball up off the rack with ease.

There is no guideline that can match your weight to how heavy your ball should be. I've seen some very small people handle a 16-pound ball with ease. The lightest regular on the PBA Tour, Chris Warren (5'5", 115 pounds) generates incredible pin action with his 16-pound ball.

Among the LPBT standouts is Donna Adamek. She's nicknamed "Mighty Mite" for good reason. Although Donna is even smaller than Chris, she has no problem controlling a heavy ball. In fact, she throws it pretty hard.

On the other hand, a lot of otherwise strong adults suffer from wrist or shoulder ailments that make using a 16-pound ball a foolhardy invitation to greater injury.

It all depends on the individual. That's yet another area in which the experienced pro will provide value for your money. By asking the right questions and by observing your actions, the pro is most likely to recommend the best weight for you.

Given the choice, it is better to err by picking a ball that is too light rather than one that is too heavy. The latter could cause bad habits, like dropping your shoulder. A one-pound error in either direction won't make a big difference.

With very rare exceptions, pros use the legal maximum of 16 pounds. The heavier the ball, the less it will deflect when crashing into the pins. Less deflection in general means better carrying power for more strikes. More strikes means more money in the bank.

There are some lane conditions in which a pro will actually reverse that principle. Most urethane balls are designed to hit like a tank. For them not to deflect at all can result in one of the modern taps; the 8- or 9-pin leave. When I won the 1991 Firestone Tournament of Champions, all but Scott Devers among the title round players used a 15-pound ball. Some Tour standouts who often go that route include Aulby, Monacelli, Miller, Benoit, and Rick Steelsmith.

If you are a power player who competes on lanes that are dry or have light pins, make note of which single-pin leave is your most common. If it is the 8 or 9 pin, consider using a lighter ball. However, the overwhelming majority of players are better off using the heaviest ball that their strength allows.

Younger players, as well as many women and most senior citizens, are far less likely to be able to derive any benefit from using a heavier ball. Added carrying power won't be of much value to you if your ball's weight causes you to miss the pocket more frequently.

If you can handle a heavier ball, go for it. Use the most weight that you can control comfortably. But don't forget

*Two-time Bowler of the Year and former PBA Rookie of the Year Mike Aulby sometimes uses a 15-pound ball.*
Courtesy American Bowling Congress

the key item: buy that ball from an expert who will make certain that you get your money's worth.

## OLD RELIABLE

You can say this for rubber bowling balls, they last forever. I have seen many league bowlers using balls that were manufactured during the 1950s.

As with every other sport, bowling equipment has come a long way since then. Golfers who once used wooden drivers now have ones featuring metal and graphite shafts. You just about have to visit the Tennis Hall of Fame to find a wooden racket. It will still get the ball over the net but it won't do it with anywhere near the efficiency, consistency, or ease of motion that is in evidence when using today's superior equipment.

The bowling balls of the 1990s are weapons compared to what existed back in the 1950s. Those light hits that would once leave the bucket (2-4-5-8 for right-handed players or 3-5-6-9 for lefties) now are more likely to be either a strike or a simple 2-pin (3-pin) conversion. There are far fewer deflection splits (examples for righties: the 5-7 and 8-10; for lefties: the 5-10 and 7-9) than ever before.

Obviously, being able to impart sufficient ball revolutions so that your shot drives through the headpin is still a prerequisite for maximum carry. But even most middle-of-the-road players can gain from what urethane offers.

As stated before, there is no need to part with $130 for your first ball. But if you intend to attack bowling seriously, the least expensive urethane models make sense. For about $20 more than a plastic ball's price you will get added potential striking power that will be unleashed as soon as you learn how to better roll your shots.

Another factor is that even a rubber ball wears down somewhat with age. Given a certain consistency of motion during our deliveries, most bowlers roll their ball over roughly the same area every time. The section of the ball that comes in contact with the lane is known as the track area.

After you have rolled a shot, observe your ball closely. You will notice that an oil ring has been transferred from the lane onto your ball's surface as it rolled toward the pins. This is your track.

After wiping off the oil with a towel, you will see a deterioration of the track area on a ball that has some miles on it. Softer surface balls, especially plastic, and balls used in centers in which the lanes are poorly maintained or oiled lightly, tend to have more nicks in them. When the track becomes very worn it's probably time to get a new ball.

Skidding causes a track to occur. The normal shot pattern is skid-roll-hook. My shots skid through the front (head) portion of the lane, much like a tire does when you slam on your brakes on a wet road. If delivered correctly, the ball will begin to roll before starting to hook toward the pocket.

Straight shooters have a skid-roll pattern. But bowlers who throw the ball too fast skid it almost the entire length of the alley. The more skid, the more wear and tear to both the lane and the ball. That's especially true when the ball is skidding on the back end of the lane, because most houses only oil the front section. There is no lubricant between the ball and the lane to minimize the stress on both.

In theory, if you rolled your shots very slowly your ball would experience virtually no deterioration.

The life expectancy of your ball will depend in large part on how you throw it and where you bowl. On the PBA Tour the lane maintenance crew uses enough oil to cover a few Alaskan beaches. That's because they want to make striking as challenging as possible to prevent pros from shooting astronomical scores.

A positive result from all that oil is that I can use the same ball longer than I could if competing under house conditions. I roll around a thousand competitive games a year (that's roughly the equivalent of participating in one league per week for about 10 years). Although each ball's life varies, I rarely use one for more than six months before it must be retired.

Ironically, the more expensive balls are not necessarily those with the greatest life expectancy. Those old rubber spheres were like rocks. You could throw one down Main Street and not hurt it. The plastic and urethane models—especially those with softer surfaces—are designed for maximum performance but not for longevity.

## TAKING CARE OF YOUR EQUIPMENT

Having spent a small fortune to buy a ball, it makes sense to take proper care to protect your investment. Never leave it in the trunk of your car during extreme weather conditions. Texas-style summer heat can cause a plastic ball to develop a flat spot if it sits for an excessive period of time. The same can happen to a lesser degree to urethane balls.

In Maine in December a ball can become brittle. Bitter cold can cause cracks to develop.

It happens every winter. Some new bowler goes running out to his car in six inches of snow to get a pack of cigarettes. With his shoes still dripping wet, he steps onto the approach for a shot that will end with him doing a fine impersonation of Greg Louganis.

You can bet your rent money that someone else will bowl after stepping in soda or catsup or the like. You can also be certain that they won't make that same mistake twice. Until it becomes legal to hit the pins with your forehead, I'd leave the diving headers to soccer players.

Not taking care of your equipment can cost you a lot more than a few pins on the scoresheet. A foreign substance on the bottom of either shoe—particularly your sliding foot—can lead to a serious injury.

Rule Number 1: Don't bring food or drink into the settee area. If there is a spill, get it cleaned up immediately.

Rule Number 2: Make every attempt never to foul. The lane oil starts at the line. Stepping in oil on this shot will get it on the bottom of your shoe, which could lead to an uncomfortable result on your subsequent delivery. You also won't be doing a service to your fellow bowlers since you will track oil onto the approach. The next player who steps in that section is in for a less-than-welcome surprise.

Which brings us to Rule Number 3: Even if you ignore Rules 1 and 2, remember to check the bottoms of your shoes before every shot. As soon as I step onto the approach I gently rub my sliding shoe on the lane. If it sticks, I put the ball down and wipe the bottom of that shoe with my towel.

After a while, this will become a subconscious part of your preshot routine. You'd be surprised how many players who ought to know better fail to take this simple yet important precaution. The time to find out that something is stuck to your shoe is before you are ready to throw the ball onto the lane and not after the lane has thrown you onto the ball.

After stepping in a sticky substance, rubbing your foot onto the approach may solve the problem. If it doesn't, rub some cigarette ashes onto the sole. I have seen numerous players apply steel wool to the problem spot. If anything, that adds to the problem by increasing the friction between

*Wiping the bottom of your sliding shoe is one preventive maintenance step that can help you to avoid a nasty fall.* Dan Chidester

the lane and your shoe. I would recommend steel wool if you step in something that's extremely sticky, such as gum.

Should the foreign item be of the slippery variety— such as baby powder—I'd use a steel wool–like substance to roughen the shoe's bottom.

Keep in mind that rules prohibit the introduction of powder to your shoes. Because it changes the surface of the approach by making it more slippery, it is dangerous to you and your fellow bowlers.

The worst bowling accident I witnessed occurred during the Pro-Am segment of a PBA tournament in my hometown of Beaumont. A player had unknowingly stepped in oil on his previous shot. He went flying on his subsequent delivery, and he suffered three fractures in his back.

## GOOD SHOES MAKE A BIG DIFFERENCE

Some centers, especially those with synthetic lane surfaces, have slippery approaches. Others are sticky, including synthetics on days when the humidity is high. When competing on either extreme, the soles of your shoes take on added importance.

When your shoes don't grip the lane, you endanger yourself. At the very least, without sufficient leverage you will be unable to transfer power from your legs to the ball.

Many bowlers tend to take their shoes for granted. As someone who endorses a specific brand (Dexter Shoes), I have become sufficiently well versed regarding that topic to understand the importance of purchasing the pair that best suits your needs. With the wrong shoes even the world's best ball will be of little help to your game. Knowing the characteristics of the center in which you bowl before buying your footwear will help you purchase the pair that best suits your needs.

My favorite pair features interchangeable soles. I carry eight or nine different slide soles, which gives me a great edge over opponents who neglect this aspect of their equipment. There have been tournaments in which some of my rivals were so concerned about whether they could execute a good (and safe) slide that they couldn't concentrate on shot making. Meanwhile, I knew my slide would be fine, allowing me to expend my mental powers on more significant matters.

Ashes, as noted, can help somewhat to alleviate a minor stick. However, they rub into the lane when used excessively, which can make the approach dangerously slippery. Consider their use to be a one-time remedy. If you find that your foot is sticking on every shot, there are alternative strategies.

One option that's popular on the Tour is to take a piece or two of a Shur-Out, a Teflon item that's meant to be inserted in the thumbhole to help your thumb exit from the ball. But it's also useful when secured to the bottom of your shoe. In time, however, the Shur-Out will deteriorate, leaving a gluelike substance remaining. At that point you will need to add another strip or remove it altogether with alcohol.

Another adjustment that PBA and LPBT players face is when the approaches seem like an ice-skating rink. Many pros opt for rubber matting that's approximately one-eighth of an inch thick to combat slippery surfaces. It helps to grip the lane better.

## DRESS FOR SUCCESS

The modern bowling shirt bears little resemblance to yesteryear's polyester version. Today's garments are fashionable items that look just like those you would wear for a few sets of tennis or for a round of golf.

It is important that the shirt does not restrict your armswing. If you opt for a cotton shirt, get the type with some give to it. Your clothing should allow for full freedom of movement.

Your pants should look nice and have a sufficiently loose fit to allow for a deep knee bend. It's great to look good but your top priority isn't to make a fashion statement. It's to knock over as many pins as you can.

## BAG THOSE BALLS

A bowling bag can be purchased for $15. Or you can spend 10 times that amount.

Here too is a case in which there is a direct correlation between price tag and life expectancy. While there is no need to spend more than half what you'd pay for a top-of-the-line bag, you shouldn't practice false economy if you want your bag to last.

Most bags are designed to hold one ball. Given that more and more serious players bring more than one ball to the lanes with them, an ever-increasing percentage of bag sales are for models that are designed to carry two balls.

Either way, quality counts. What looks good on the shelf may not look so hot two years from now. A good tip is to observe how much attention to detail the manufacturer has given to a specific model. Are the zippers metallic or nylon? Have the handles been sewn onto the bag or were they riveted? Is the shape of the bag designed to aid stability?

To most of us, a zipper is a zipper. That's what I once thought. But I have found that the newer type made of nylon seems to last a lot longer with a lot fewer problems than the older style. Handles attached with a needle and thread are far more likely to become dislodged than those connected by rivets.

The bottom of the bag should be wider than the top. If it's not, expect it to fly around in the trunk of your car. Needless to say, that won't do your ball, your car, or your bag's longevity a lot of good.

You can usually determine the thickness of its materials by feeling the bag. Except for the best of the best, bags are no longer made from leather. Soft nylon or cordura are prevalent. Either way, if the outside of the bag seems thin, you can be sure that model hasn't been designed to last very long.

Your bowling bag should have a separate compartment for your shoes (so they aren't squashed under the weight of your ball). There should also be an area for your basic accessories: rosin bag, scissors, bowler's tape, an extra set of shoelaces and the like.

In addition to a sturdy handle, double bags should also have a shoulder strap. Between two balls and your accessories, a full double bag will weigh around 35 pounds. It is a lot easier to carry that over your shoulder than from an extended arm.

Another relatively new feature is that some bags allow you to remove the inner liner so that it can be washed.

Durability is a concern. One customer of mine came into our pro shop after his dog had done a number on his bag. Although there were teeth marks everywhere, the bag had held up remarkably well. For what it's worth, his model was made out of a thin, parachutelike material.

The price range for single bags is around $15 to $50. The least expensive double bag runs about $30.

Add to that owning two balls ($250), a good pair of shoes ($70), and various accessories ($20–30) and you have a sizeable investment. Perhaps as a pro shop proprietor I'm prejudiced, so take the following advice with whatever credence you wish to attach to it. After spending so much, it's silly to practice false economy by buying anything less than the ball or shoes that best serve your needs.

I can't stress sufficiently that your most important decision won't be what to buy, but where you buy it. At the Winner's Edge, as with virtually all bowling center pro shops, we sell nothing except bowling equipment. My knowledge of ball drilling can give my customers a big edge in both comfort and function over those who go the department store route.

# 4
# *Striking It Rich*

It's easy to strike out in baseball or in your job, your social life, or with life in general. So how come it's only in bowling—which is supposed to be such a simple game—that striking out is so difficult?

While virtually anyone can get lucky and roll a strike, the ability to string those *X*s together on a consistent basis is far from easy. Such is the nature of the sport's scoring system that a premium is placed on the ability to clear the deck on your first shot. Roll several consecutive strikes and you'll post some significant numbers.

Without the benefit of a double you will have to achieve a decent count on your shots after rolling a spare, and mark in 7 of 10 frames just to bowl in the 150s. The formula for filling frames changes dramatically in your favor if you have the ability to string your strikes together.

Each consecutive strike rolled represents two fewer spares you will need to achieve the same score. Produce a four-bagger and you can score as high as a 162 *without* even a single spare! Of course, a few conversions will really give you great results. Marry four straight strikes with just

***The strike: not as easy as it looks!*** Dan Chidester

three spares in the other half-dozen frames and optimum pin count rises to 193!

There are two types of strikes in bowling: excellent shots and the lucky variety. I define an excellent shot as a strike thrown by me. The lucky strike is any thrown by my opponent.

I'm only half joking about the above, because a certain amount of chance is involved anytime you are able to carry your strike shot attempt. We have all seen seemingly horrible nose hits set off a weird succession of pins toppling awkwardly into one another until none remains standing. I have even witnessed strikes in which the ball missed the headpin altogether! We all know the agony of being robbed (or, as it's called in bowling, tapped) after placing our shot right in the pocket.

Human nature being what it is, when I catch a break I usually just think of it as justice being done to make up for an earlier misfortune. But if an opponent gets lucky, well, that's a different matter!

Over the long run, luck tends to even out. When it doesn't run your way you have to accept it as the rub of the green. As a pro I have learned that luck doesn't play nearly as big a role as we would like to believe after we have suffered a defeat.

I still recall the viewpoint offered to me years ago by then-Touring pro Bill Straub. Now the varsity bowling coach at the University of Nebraska, Bill preaches that there is no such thing as bad luck, there's only bad roll. If you are able to obtain good leverage at the point of release you will find a lot more breaks headed your way.

*David struck in eight of the first nine frames of the 1991 title game when he defeated Monacelli 236-203 for pro bowling's most coveted title, the Firestone Tournament of Champions.* Russ Vitale

The majority of what pass for taps are really the result of small mistakes made by the bowler. It's important that you come to understand why some shots carry and others don't if you are to make corrections and achieve long-term improvement in your strike game (to say nothing of maintaining your sanity).

*Dave's ball enters the 1-3 pocket to set off the chain reaction that rockets 10 pins into the pit.* Dan Chidester

## THE CHAIN REACTION

Before we discuss why that nasty 10 pin refused to fall after your ball exploded into the pocket, let's cover what is supposed to occur.

First, you want your ball to impact on the opposite side of the headpin from the trajectory of your shot. In other words, a ball that is angled from right to left should be aimed at the right side of the headpin and vice versa. Left-handed bowlers use the 1-2 pocket while righties aim for the 1-3 zone.

The so-called crossover—or Brooklyn—strike results when your shot carries after crossing in front of the headpin to impact against the "wrong" pocket. Missing your target by a considerable margin only to be rewarded with a strike can be devastating to your opponent. Whenever I carry a Brooklyn hit I consider it a bonus, like scoring an unearned run in baseball. All players will be so blessed a certain percent of the time.

Let's say you've thrown a Brooklyn strike. Should you attempt to duplicate your motions and your target on subsequent shots, or is an adjustment the better route?

I always opt for the latter. Crossing in front of that headpin is bowling's version of Russian roulette. There are just too many dangers involved to do so intentionally.

Having carried a crossover hit can give you a mental lift. In some cases, it can spur a player to victory. Del Ballard, Jr., won his eighth title when he came from behind against Mike Shady in the championship game of the 1991 Kessler Open. His rally was sparked by a Brooklyn hit that was the first of four consecutive strikes. Shady, who had struck in three of the first four frames, was far less effective afterward.

Later, Del admitted that he had been tentative at the start of the game. He stated that his crossover shot had made him mad. Said Del, "I told myself, 'I'm better than that.' "

The psychological impact of tossing a Brooklyn strike notwithstanding, it's far better to be in the "right" pocket. As a rule, carry percentage is far greater. Those who roll a back-up ball (also known as a reverse curve) use the opposite pocket.

The reason that the pocket of choice works best has to do with the number-one enemy of the strike ball—deflection.

Ball deflection represents to the bowler what spinach is to a seven-year-old who must eat it to get dessert. The rest of the menu, no matter how delectable, is quickly forgotten, and only a sour taste (and a lot of whining) remains.

When your ball is unduly deflected by the headpin, it becomes impossible for the pins to carry out the desired chain reaction. That's why people who bemoan their luck over long periods of time are only kidding themselves.

"How come Joe barely touches the headpin and gets a strike and I'm in the pocket every frame and only get nine," they cry. "It just isn't fair."

The answer is that Joe's ball was rolled in a manner that generates greater inertia to avoid deflection. Producing strikes consistently requires a combination of accuracy and power. One without the other is as undesirable as being stuck with spinach when you don't have a dog under the table to sneak it to.

Believe it or not, on the perfect strike your ball will only make direct contact with four central pins. The remainder of the rack must be eliminated by wood toppling wood. But wood would only whack wood if wood could. Which is where our old enemy of deflection is again a factor.

The accompanying photograph illustrates the two clas-

**The four Impact Pins (in white) are the only ones that actually come in contact with the ball during an ideal pocket hit. The remaining six sticks (dark) are the Chain Reaction Pins.** Dan Chidester

sifications of pins. The regular (white) ones are the impact pins (which we will refer to as IP). These are the ones that are actually knocked over directly by your ball.

We have colored the remaining half-dozen sticks. These are the chain reaction pins (CRP). As you can see, five of them are located on the outside flanks of the rack.

In the diagram on page 89, shot A is the sort of hit most commonly associated with right-handed players and with the occasional southpaw who uses a back-up ball. The shot's path moves from right to left as it enters the 1-3 pocket. What is important is that your shot continues along virtually the same path unabated after it has collided with the headpin.

If that is the case, your ball will then drive into the 5-9 combo with the 5 pin sliding into the 8 pin. The 3 pin takes out the 6, which in turn hits the 10 pin. Meanwhile, the headpin will have hit the 2 pin. The 2 pin will meet up with the 4 pin, which eliminates the 7 pin.

Ball line B shows the mirror image of the perfect strike for those of you who are either left-handed or are right-handed and employ a back-up ball. In this case your desired pocket is between the 1 and the 2 pins. The ball again drives into the 5 pin, which takes out the 9 as the ball proceeds through to the 8 pin. The same sort of chain reaction occurs on the flank sticks so that an *X* is achieved.

A strike can also result should your ball stray just across to the "wrong" side of the headpin. But there is danger when you live on the so-called Brooklyn side. If your shot doesn't go far enough across, the subsequent nose hit will probably leave you faced with one of bowling's "impossible" splits.

You will also suffer should your ball drift even slightly too far to the opposite pocket. Because your ball is now moving away from the center of the rack upon impact, it will be deflected well wide of the 5 pin. I have actually seen some of these hits conclude with the ball leaving the alley over the spot where the far corner pin was placed.

Such massive deflection is likely to leave you with a

**Strike Lines >**

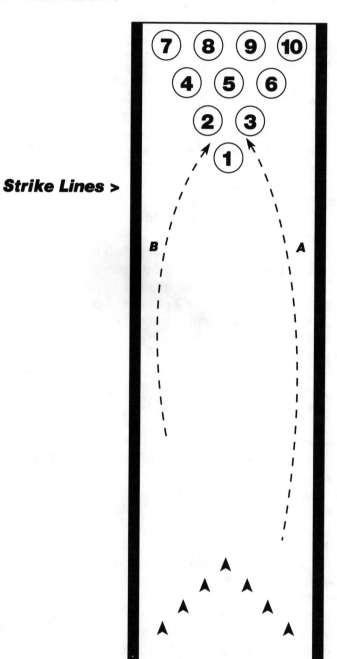

split like the 5-10 (for Line A–type players) or the 5-7 (Line B players).

Regardless of which hand you use or how you roll your shot, it is important to avoid hitting the middle of the headpin. In that case the 2 and 3 pins are sent too far sideways. Instead of the IPs setting off an effective chain reaction, they will be projected at an undesirable angle and will likely slide harmlessly out of play. The result is often a split that resembles Grandpa's teeth (a few on each side with nothing in between).

Barring a conversion that borders on the miraculous, an open frame will be your punishment for leaves such as the 7-10, 4-6, 4-6-7-10, 4-6-7, 6-7-10, 4-6-7-9-10, 4-6-7-8-10. The first three of these are considered "impossible" splits. With 180-degree angle involved between pins, it takes the shot of a lifetime to convert any of these leaves.

All of the above, except in some cases the 7-10, occurred because your lack of accuracy allowed your shot to drift "high." The 7-10 can also occur on a light pocket hit. Nose hits—whether delivered by Joe Frazier in a boxing ring or by one of us on a lane—are painful experiences.

## POWER TO THE PEOPLE

Some splits are caused by insufficient power. It's like when a small child rolls a lightweight ball at slow speed. The ball nudges the headpin, barely convincing it to fall. Having done that much, the ball lazily drifts sideways toward the gutter. Sometimes it just stops in the middle of the pin deck.

While the typical adult isn't so dramatically lacking when it comes to imparting the necessary amount of inertia, many lower-average players nonetheless need to greatly improve their ball speed. You need to roll your shot firmly without flinging it.

Too much speed is no bargain, either, from the perspectives of both carry and accuracy. Proper timing, balance, and leverage are virtually impossible to maintain when using an unnatural delivery in an ill-advised attempt to obtain more speed than you can naturally control.

Contrary to popular misconception, speed does not equal power, even though a lack of adequate speed will cost you power. Remember that 60 percent of the pins are in the CRP category. It is crucial that the front two IPs (the 1-3 for those of you covered by Line A and the 1-2 for you who consulted Line B) set into motion a series of movements in which pins fly into—*not* over—one another.

A rocket that explodes into wood looks and sounds impressive. If it goes too fast it can cause pins to "toe up." The bottom (toe) of the pin is lifted skyward. Instead of the 6 hitting the 10 pin or the 4 hitting the 7 pin, the lower-numbered stick may fly around the neck of the corner pin.

For optimum results, we pros work on having enough speed coupled with a desirable roll to avoid deflection. We're equally careful to avoid throwing our strike shots too hard. Excessive speed is no bargain.

Power comes from imparting an optimum roll pattern on your ball as it proceeds down the lane, *not* from how fast you have projected your shot. The ideal shot skids through the (oiled) front segment of the lane before going into a roll. As it nears the pins it begins to hook toward the pocket. This skid-roll-hook sequence is a very important component of the carrying formula.

A ball that begins to hook prematurely will *roll out* before it collides with the headpin. In plain English, that means it will have expended most of its energy and inertia on the lane and have precious little left for overpowering the pins.

Del Ballard, Jr., and Amleto Monacelli are two superstars who know how to use rollout to their advantage on certain lane conditions. Amleto's unique release allows his ball to explode into the pocket, yet it seems to always roll out before sailing high. His ability to do that has made him one of bowling's all-time top performers.

Their success notwithstanding, rollout is bowling's equivalent to those cars you see racing across curved mountain roads during commercials, in which the fine print tells us that we're seeing a professional driver on a closed track and that we shouldn't try this ourselves. Except in the hands of an experienced pro bowler, rollout can lead to danger.

There is much talk among better players about their *break point*. Break point refers to the distance the ball is from the pins when it begins to hook. A ball that breaks too soon is likely to deflect. One that breaks too late will enter the pocket at a steep angle. It's said to come from "behind" the headpin, which increases the odds of a corner pin (or two) remaining.

Bowlers who roll a ball with a big hook find an inside line to their advantage, since it decreases the angle of pocket entry. Just as with excessive speed, a steep entry angle or a ball that hooks too late are less likely to carry the corner pins.

For my purposes, I like it when my ball goes about three-quarters of the way down the lane before veering toward the pocket. If my shot is going "long," I can use less ball speed to make it break sooner. Another option is to change the positioning of my fingers during my release point from 5 o'clock to an "earlier" time (such as 3 or 4 o'clock). Or you can change your ball.

Conversely, an increase in speed will make the ball break later. So will staying behind the ball more during the release instead of rotating my hand in a counterclockwise direction.

Among better bowlers there is much talk of how many "revs" a player generates. Ball revolutions are a key to maximizing your striking power. If you closely observe a professional power player you will note that his or her shots "rev up." Not only will their ball revolve 15+ times as it goes down the lane, it will achieve the majority of those revs after entering its hooking pattern on the back end of the alley.

The joke on Tour is that Amleto Monacelli's shots experience more revolutions than a banana republic.

Balls that are fitted with bright-colored finger grips

*Lisa Wagner's great strike ball has helped the LPBT great to win more pro titles than any other player in the history of women's pro bowling.* Courtesy of Brunswick Corporation

make it easy to keep track of how many revs you have obtained on a shot. I wouldn't advise you to worry about revs until such time as you can comfortably hook the ball. Ball revs, as they apply to your game, will be maximized by executing the fundamental steps to the best of your ability.

There is a correlation between velocity and revs. Too much speed means your ball will skid too far down the lane before achieving its roll-hook pattern. As a result, you will lose much of your shot's tracking ability and you will sacrifice revs.

Insufficient speed will bring about early hook, in which your ball will roll out before it finishes its journey. Having expended too much of its energy too early, it will be DOA (dead on arrival). It will actually stop hooking before it meets the headpin and will weakly deflect on impact.

Nevertheless, a certain minimum amount of speed is

required. Your ability to prevent excess deflection is how to avoid being confronted with splits such as the 5-7, 5-10, 8-10, and 7-9. An added benefit from generating a minimum acceptable amount of speed is the opportunity to make use of the sidewalls, whose deflection of pins back onto the deck will greatly upgrade your carrying ability.

How do you know if you are rolling the ball too slowly or too fast? You can have a teammate observe your game to see if your shots are rolled significantly harder or softer than those of most of the better bowlers in your league. You can also feel if you are out of balance from trying to roll your shots too hard. Finally, you can use a stopwatch.

Have a friend time how long it takes your ball to reach the headpin after you have released your shot. That 60-foot distance should be covered in no less than two seconds and no more than three. If there is any such thing as an ideal strike ball speed, it's probably found in the neighborhood of 2.4 to 2.5 seconds.

That isn't to say that you *must* be in that range. Mike Aulby is a certain future Hall of Fame member and his shots take much longer than that to reach their destination. Dave Ferraro, the 1990 Firestone Tournament of Champions winner, usually rolls his shots far faster than my preferred range. The key to ball speed is to be consistent and to find the amount of velocity that works best with your type of release and roll.

Keep in mind, too, that the amount of conditioner on the lane and the type of ball that you're using affect speed. The more oil and the softer the surface of your ball, the more speed is lost. It's not unusual to see a decrease of around three miles per hour from the head (front end) portion of the lane until the ball reaches the pindeck on a wet lane.

A hooking (dry) lane is more likely to absorb your ball's energy to cause rollout. Your shot stops skidding and starts to roll earlier, which in turn makes for an earlier hook. Increasing speed will make your shot skid more to counteract this condition.

**The amount of conditioner applied to a lane affects how your ball will react.** Dan Chidester

## USING THE SIDEWALLS TO FULL ADVANTAGE

Just as there is said to be more than one way to skin the proverbial cat, there are different varieties of strikes. The so-called wall shot results when your ball doesn't deflect on a light hit. By its "driving through," the headpin will ricochet back into play to topple the three remaining pins.

Because your shot was light, the headpin sailed in front of the 2 pin en route to colliding with the left sidewall (or, in the case of left-handed players, the headpin flew in front of the 3 pin before deflecting off the right sidewall). If your ball had been rolled weakly, the headpin would have remained in the gutter. But by executing a good release, you caused the headpin to eliminate the 4-5-7 combination (for a righty) or the 5-6-10 (for a lefty).

The headpin also comes into play on the so-called messenger hit. That's when a 10 pin remains after a light hit. The headpin hits the opposite sidewall and rolls across the lane before tripping the 10 pin (the 7 pin for left-handers).

These are two more examples of why a modicum of speed is advantageous. Anything slower would not enable you to exploit one of the bowler's best friends—the lively sidewall. These barriers are great for sending pins back into play to eliminate wood. The wall shot and the messenger strikes are not lucky shots.

People who roll a back-up ball very rarely benefit from such hits. Conversely, bowlers who roll a powerful hook ball are able to widen the pocket by virtue of the level of inertia their shots enjoy as a result.

Another common strike in the modern game is the rip rack. Once again, a light hit is rewarded. This time the ball barely touches the 5 pin, but your shot has enough power to drive the 5 into the 7 pin. It's a nice shot to carry but it also tells you that you're living dangerously. The difference between a rip rack strike and suffering a blowout 7-10 split is slight.

## DEFLECTION SPLITS AND SPARES

The 1960s expression "speed kills" applies, but a much more damaging phenomenon is that deflection is murder on your game. There are a series of leaves that are caused by this one major malady, starting with the soft corner pin leave (the 7 pin for you Line B types, the 10 pin for the rest of us).

Remember that we want your ball to hit against the near side of the headpin combined with the left side of the 3 pin (Line A) or the right side of the 2 pin (Line B players). Excessive deflection means that instead of that happening, your ball will contact more toward the center portion of the other stick. The 3 pin (for a righty) or the 2 pin (for a lefty) is then sent backward instead of to the side. In turn, that pin will then cause the 4 pin (righty) or the 6 pin (lefty) to lazily fall in front of the corner pin.

Another possibility is that your ball will either barely touch the 5 pin or will fail to hit it altogether. In the former case, the 5 will slide in front of either the 8 pin (Line A) or the 9 pin (Line B).

The 8-10 and 7-9 splits are the result of a shot that had far too little juice. They occurred because your thumb either went downward or remained in the ball too long. Either way, your fingers lost the opportunity to impart the necessary lift on the ball to produce a powerful roll. Any of the deflection leaves means that you—not a lack of luck— were to blame.

Another contributing factor could be tight back ends. This results when the lane conditioner has carried down from the front part of the lane to the back portion. Oil retards friction (and with it your shot's hook). Tight back ends make it difficult to avoid deflection. Your adjustment

*When all else fails, a little body English can't hurt. All-time star Marshall Holman's game features a great ball roll that has helped him become one of a handful of pros to have won more than 20 titles.* Courtesy of Brunswick Corporation

is to use less speed and to redouble your concentration on executing a good release.

Bowling's easiest spare leave is also a member of the deflection-caused category. There is a saying among players: "No drive, no five." A weak hit will leave you with only that central stick, if you're fortunate. If you aren't so lucky, the 5-7 or the 5-10 will remain.

With an eye back on you Line A folks, let's see how the 5-7 results. After contacting against the headpin, the ball veers to the right rather than driving through and into the 5 pin. The headpin goes slightly more to the left than the norm. Instead of hitting the side of the 2 pin it hits the front of that stick. The 2 pin is driven more backward than sideways so that the very inside of the 4 pin is contacted. The 4 travels around the front of the 7 pin instead of driving into it.

The 5-10 is the Line B player's equivalent.

The amount of deflection often determines the extent of the damage. Your ball should deflect slightly. The only true taps in modern bowling are the 8 pin (right-handed players) or the 9 pin (left-handed players). These are caused by a hook ball that is so powerful that it doesn't deflect after hitting the headpin. As a result, the 5 pin is driven directly backward rather than going sideways to take out the 8 or the 9 pin.

The first time you are faced with this should be viewed as something of a milestone. It's like getting a speeding ticket while driving an antique car. It's a dubious distinction but a badge of honor nonetheless.

Little or no deflection should mean a strike in most instances. A bit more deflection will often leave you with a single-pin leave, usually a corner pin. Excessive deflection causes the sort of split configurations we discussed.

The most common deflection spare is the 10 pin (for the player whose shot is illustrated by Line A) or the 7 pin (for those covered by Line B). There is a big difference between a "ringing" 7 or 10 pin and the "soft" variety.

The former results when the nearest CRP flies around

the corner stick. The soft variety is when that same CRP dies harmlessly in the gutter in front of the corner pin. A ringing leave means you made a fairly good shot only to suffer just the smallest amount of excess deflection. You can feel slightly unlucky in this case although you were not robbed.

The soft variety is definitely not a function of bad luck. Your ball deflected significantly, which is why you are now shooting a spare instead of accepting your teammates' congratulations.

It is important that you watch your ball intently as it enters the pin deck to determine not just what you have left, but also *why* those pins are still standing. Did your ball power through the rack after hitting the pocket, or did it weakly ricochet to the side? The knowledge you gain can be put to good use on subsequent shots. Merely knowing that you left the 10 pin isn't sufficient. You need to analyze why it failed to fall to determine if you need to make an adjustment on your next delivery, and if so what type of adjustment will work the best.

A ringing leave is just one of those things. Consider it to be an occupational hazard. The soft leave calls for making a change. Remember, your job doesn't end when that ball leaves your hand. Not only are you a bowler, you are also your own coach. As such, you need to be observant.

To adjust, you must move your feet in the same direction that you missed while maintaining the same target. In bowling parlance: if you miss left, move left. Thus, if you are a right-handed bowler who just rolled a Brooklyn shot, you should move your feet to the left on your subsequent delivery. More on adjustments shortly.

## OTHER COMMON SPARE LEAVES

The margin of error that separates a strike from a spare conversion attempt is often slight. The difference between tripping that 4 pin and failing to do so isn't nearly as great as you might guess.

It is important that you come to understand *why* a pin

(or a cluster of pins) fails to fall so that you can compensate on your upcoming shots. In each of the following cases I will list the Line A leave with its Line B equivalent in parentheses.

The 4-pin (6-pin) leave results when your shot drifts slightly high in the pocket. In most cases, being a board or two lighter would have meant a strike.

The 2-pin (3-pin) leave or any combination such as the 2-4-5 (3-5-6) or the bucket, which is the 2-4-5-8 (3-5-6-9), is caused by a very light hit or your ball breaking too late. You can figure that you missed the pocket by about two boards.

Often, the difference between having just the 2 pin (3) or being faced with a cluster involves how much hooking power you generate. It's very rare when a Pete Weber or an Amleto Monacelli has to convert the bucket because they possess what bowlers refer to as a working ball.

The baby split is the 3-10 (2-7). Your shot went high and hit against the middle of the headpin.

## MAKING ADJUSTMENTS

On the professional bowling level we sometimes make minor adjustments to compensate for the ringing 10-pin (7-pin). In your case, I wouldn't recommend that you consider tinkering with your delivery, hand position, starting spot, or the like. Be content to hit the pocket and to make a good shot while knowing that being able to do that consistently will add up to a good score. If you make changes, the chances are that you will do more harm than good.

However, a weak leave and especially deflection splits call for revising your strategy. You need to concentrate on executing a good release so that your ball drives through the pins. In addition, move your feet one board in the direction of the gutter that's on the same side as your bowling hand. Maintain the same target on the lane. This will cause your shot to finish just slightly higher on the headpin, enough, we hope, to alleviate the problem. If not, move another board on your subsequent shot.

As a rule, always move your feet in the direction in which your shot strayed while keeping the same aiming point on the lane. When your ball goes too far to the left, move to your left. When it goes too far to the right, move to the right.

If your shot was high, move your feet a board or two toward the center on the approach. When it's light, head toward the right gutter (for right-handed players and for a lefty with a back-up ball).

Let's say you have left the 4 pin (6 pin). You know that the probable cause was that your shot was about one board high. It's up to you to determine if the problem was caused by a physical mistake that you made or whether the lane's oil pattern changed.

Your mental checklist for the former includes the following questions:

**1.** Did I hit my target on the lane?
**2.** Was my speed consistent with previous shots? (Slower speed will cause your ball to hook more, while a faster speed will make it hook less.)
**3.** Did I release the ball in a similar manner to my previous shots?

If your answers are all affirmative, then a geographical lane adjustment is appropriate. Move your feet one board toward your nonbowling hand. Line A bowlers will move left, Line B players will move to their right. This should solve the problem. Never make a move if one or more of the above responses was a no. You can only make an educated guess as to what adjustment is most appropriate after you have executed a good delivery.

Keep in mind that no two lanes are exactly alike. It's possible that the pair on which you are playing may be dissimilar. You have to keep mental tabs how shots are reacting on each lane of your pair because you may need to stand in different spots on the two approaches to get the same results.

A common adjustment on the pro Tours is called a two-

**1991 Masters champ
Doug Kent keenly
observes how his ball
reacts on the lane and
after hitting the pins to
help gain valuable
strategic insights.**
Courtesy American Bowling
Congress

and-one move. We move our feet two boards and our target one board in the same direction (both feet and target to the left or both to the right). If you move in the direction of your bowling hand (e.g., a right-handed player moving to the right) your subsequent shot will go two inches/boards higher (more to the left). Move away from your bowling hand and your next delivery will be two inches/boards lighter.

The normal move of maintaining a target results in a two-inch change for every board moved. Thus, moving your feet two boards to the left means that your next shot should end up four inches/boards more to the right. These formulas hold for modest changes of a few boards.

A dramatic change such as moving from playing up the gutter to playing a deep inside line involves much guesswork and probably an accompanying change in equipment, release, and ball speed. If that sounds complex it's because it is just that. Only the most experienced of pros might attempt such a move and only then as a last resort when scoring badly.

As a rule, the more to the outside you stand the more the ball will hook. Thus, a right-handed player who is positioned near the right gutter can expect his or her shot to end its skid and begin to roll, then hook, both more and sooner. The more the right-hander moves to his or her left (or a lefty moves right), the longer the shot is likely to slide and the less it will hook.

Just because you rolled a strike does not mean that you are properly lined up. I can stand anywhere on a lane and get a strike if I execute all of my movements to perfection. The trick to learning how to read a lane to line up properly is to find the combination of release, ball speed, type of equipment, and angle to the pocket that yields the greatest margin for error.

Playing the lanes correctly is as important in bowling as having the appropriate club in golf. I could no more win on the PBA Tour than Tom Watson could if he was forced to tee off on a par 5 with a 9-iron. All good golfers know how far they hit each club. They know when to add a club to compensate for a lot of carry to the green or when to subtract one if the wind is at their back.

The art of lining up in bowling involves knowing your own game, reading the lane condition, and observing what others are doing. In some ways, our chore is tougher than that of our golfing counterparts. They can see their pitfalls. Our sand traps are invisible. I can't tell by looking if the lane has a dry spot or a small puddle of oil. Golfers know the exact distance between their ball and the hole. I must make my best guess at what's between me and the pins.

Guess right and you'll be rewarded. It's not uncommon to hear a pro bowler refer to a competitor's high scores by saying that his rival "had five boards to play with." Translation: That player could miss his target by five boards and still strike.

The antithesis of that is having to "split boards." That's when you must be inch-perfect to hit the pocket or carry.

**Veteran pro Dave Husted is among the game's most knowledgeable players, which helps him to get lined up quickly and correctly.** Courtesy Professional Bowlers Association

It doesn't take an Einstein to calculate that the greater your margin for error, the more success you will enjoy.

Most Tour veterans have found another few pros whose games are similar enough to their own to be able to learn from how they're playing the lane. Personally, I often line up off Brian Voss and Dave Husted.

I won the 1986 Lite Beer Classic in Miami thanks to following Voss's lead. It was at Don Carter's Kendall Lanes that I had gotten off to a terrible start. After the initial six-game qualifying block I noticed that Voss was firing bullets up the first arrow. I decided to give that approach a try. The next thing I knew, I was leading the field by a comfortable margin.

There are players whose style might appear to be similar to mine but whose release and roll make it virtually impossible to glean any knowledge about playing the lanes from watching them. Steve Wunderlich falls into that cate-

***The author's win in Miami in 1986 was made possible by
stealing Brian Voss's strategy.*** Courtesy Brunswick Corporation

gory. When Steve and I won the 1990 Showboat/PBA Doubles Classic he was playing a deep inside line and I was
playing the edge of the gutter.

That we could use such different strategies but both
enjoy a positive result shows that there is no one right line,
ball, speed, or release for everyone. That's why I recommend that you find someone in your league whose game is
similar to yours whom you can observe. You may be able to
"go to school" on those occasions when he or she is using
different tactics than you and he or she is knocking 'em
dead while you are struggling.

With time, you will probably discover the combination
that tends to yield the best results in the center in which
you most often bowl. That's a good starting point for future

outings, but it doesn't mean you should become locked into that as your only line.

What to do when rolling in a strange house? That's an issue that we pros face on a weekly basis. Some players will try their favorite shot first. My recommendation is that you stand on the center dot and use the second arrow as your target. If you are a big hook player, aim instead for the first arrow. Adjust from there based on how your ball reacts and by what you see others with similar games to yours are successfully doing.

The difference between winning and losing on Tour is often not only the ability to analyze, but to make the proper decision a game or two ahead of your rivals. There have been many pros who have enjoyed successful careers whose physical skills were subpar by PBA or LPBT standards. Conversely, I've seen some physically gifted players who couldn't cut it on Tour because their mental game was lacking.

Ted Hannahs and Joe Hutchinson both do almost everything wrong. Ted's footwork wanders across the lane and his armswing goes in more directions than a skid-row drunk. In fact, he likes to joke that he would win every week if everyone was forced to try to bowl with his style.

Although Ted and Joe don't have textbook styles, they've done well for a long time. That's because both are extremely bright men who have married their intellect with a great knowledge of bowling.

Believe me, the little things they do can add up to big results. After you have achieved a certain ability level, the difference between success and failure is often more mental than physical. In bowling, as in life, knowledge is the key.

## KNOW YOUR ANGLES

What of you straight-ball shooters? If that's your style, it is vital that you also take advantage of angles. Don't roll the ball down the middle portion of the lane. Instead, stand to the side of the alley that's on the same side as your bowling arm. Right-handed players should place their feet on the far right side of the approach, just inside of the right gutter. Left-handers move to the left.

While standing at the foul line, draw an imaginary line from the shoulder on the side of your bowling arm through the pocket. Move your feet slightly to either side until that line dissects one of the arrows on the lane (preferably the first or second arrow to allow for a good angle of entry).

To find where you should be positioned during your address point (that's the spot on which you stand before you begin your delivery), simply extend that imaginary line backward. By walking along that line during your delivery you will direct all of your motions toward your target. This is extremely important if you are to execute a straight and nonrestricted armswing as already described.

You have now found the spot on the floor from which I recommend that you release your strike ball. Remember, this is a guesstimate. Through trial and error you will discover where you feel the most comfortable and get the best results.

By obtaining an angled approach to the pocket you will lessen the amount that your ball will deflect. You will also be far less likely to produce a nose hit. The result will be a greater carrying percentage (that key ratio of strikes recorded per pocket hits produced) as well as fewer splits. Eventually, as you obtain more accuracy and confidence, you will want to swap that straight shot for a hook.

That's because a ball that is curving toward the pocket enters that zone at a greater angle than does a straight ball. It also grips the lane more efficiently to generate more inertia after hitting the headpin. These traits combine to minimize ball deflection. As we know, less deflection equals more carrying power for more strikes.

A hook shot is a great weapon as long as the added power is not overshadowed by a greater loss of accuracy. A boxer's best punch doesn't count for much if it doesn't land. And all of the ball revolutions generated by the world's most powerful bowler wouldn't add up to a hill of beans if his or her shots consistently missed the pocket.

A relatively balanced combination of accuracy and power is the ideal. Some of the best strike shooters in the world don't roll huge hook balls. Conversely, there are players who can aim a ball at Maine and make it hook to Montana but who don't strike very often because they can't hit an elephant from 60 feet away.

Unfortunately for the sake of emulation, the relatively straight strike ball of a Walter Ray Williams, Jr., or a Don Genalo doesn't draw oohs and aahs from fans, while Amleto Monacelli's and Pete Weber's atomic bombs leave people in awe.

It *is* extremely impressive to watch pins virtually shatter when Pete or Amleto sends a shot hanging just over the edge of the gutter before the ball violently veers at the last possible instant into the pocket. Their awesome strike power is as exciting to the bowling fan as a Michael Jordan slam dunk is to a basketball buff or a Jose Canseco tape-measure clout is to a baseball fanatic.

What makes Pete, Amleto, and a handful of others like them so charismatic is precisely that they are so special. My entire generation of bowlers was influenced when Mark Roth and Marshall Holman revolutionized the game by showing how effective a weapon power can be when properly harnessed.

Scores of critics insisted that nobody could possibly be successful with so radical a style as Mark featured when he first hit the PBA Tour. Mark did many things that conventional wisdom said were wrong. He took too many steps. And how could he possibly be accurate with such a big hook? No, the critics all agreed, he would never survive among the world's best with an approach to the game that was so dramatically different from all of his predecessors.

Roth's greatness quickly became apparent even to those who had been so eager to dismiss his potential. Suddenly, it seemed, every young player wanted to roll the ball like him.

One quality that fans often ignore that makes Mark so great is that he can also throw a ball that's straighter than Donny Osmond. That's a key reason why he may be the

*Maybe the straight-shot style of 1986 Player of the Year Walter Ray Williams isn't as charismatic as the big hook ball, but earning $100,000+ for four consecutive years is nothing to sneeze at.*
Courtesy Professional Bowlers Association

*Mark Roth influenced an entire generation of bowlers and helped to usher in the modern power-oriented era.*
Courtesy Professional Bowlers Association

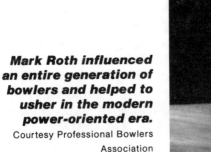

greatest spare and split shooter in the history of our sport. To be able to roll a superpowerful hook with accuracy and also have the ability to go directly at a target is a magnificent combination.

It is the result of possessing fantastic natural ability and developing that potential as a youngster by bowling at almost every opportunity. Amleto and Pete, like Mark Roth, virtually lived in a bowling center as they grew up. So did I as well as almost all of my contemporaries on both the PBA and LPBT Tours.

Another Roth asset was his unparalleled instinct for strategy. He was such a natural—both mentally and physically—that I wonder if bowling will ever see his like again.

The overwhelming majority of you readers roll fewer games in a year than we do in the typical week. Thus, to achieve the following Roth/Weber/Monacelli traits you must bowl hundreds of games a year and be blessed with great natural ability:

**1.** Cover a great number of boards with a wide hook while maintaining consistent speed to promote accuracy.

**2.** Make equipment, hand release, and lane angle adjustments based on intricate awareness of the game's nuances. This requires tremendous knowledge and skill.

**3.** Change back and forth from the big hook ball (for strike shots) to rolling a shot straight (at certain spare and split conversions).

All of the above require fantastic natural athleticism married with skill honed through countless hours of bowling. If you could master any of the above categories—much less all three—you would now be reading a book on investing to determine how to best allocate the extremely handsome income you'd be earning on the pro Tour.

Roth's example aside, you will enjoy greater success if your strike shot and your spare delivery are fairly similar. A ball that hooks 5–15 boards/inches is more than adequate

**The most powerful strike ball on the Ladies Tour probably belongs to 1991 LPBT Player of the Year Leanne Barrette.**
Courtesy Ladies Pro Bowlers Tour

for greatly increasing carry percentage compared to a straight shot. Of equal import, it won't unduly sacrifice your accuracy.

For every board you add to your hook ball you will lose a certain amount of control. The key is to find the proper balance between these two very important components to good scoring.

The majority of contemporary bowlers would happily trade a week full of Sundays for Pete or Amleto's strike ball. Unless you are committed to bowling as often as they do—and, believe me, there are times it seems that all we pros do is bowl!—you are far better advised to emulate Walter Ray or Don.

Remember: the greater distance that your strike shot hooks, the less control and consistency you are likely to enjoy. Errors in your armswing, timing, or speed control will be magnified. It is far easier to strike more often by rolling a controlled hook.

Let's take two hypothetical bowlers, each of whom I'm sure you've come across in every league in which you have participated.

Bowler A is infatuated with that big hook ball and how awed others are when he throws it just right. Three times out of four, pocket hits send pins through the roof. But Bowler A only hits his target once every three frames.

Bowler B is nowhere near as athletically gifted as her more powerful counterpart but makes up for that by concentrating on hitting the target. Only half of B's pocket hits carry. But B gets her shots into the pocket twice every three frames.

After three games, A will have eight *X*s. Player B will have rolled 10! And B will probably cover a lot more spares and suffer far fewer split leaves because of the benefits of being accurate. So Bowler A will look great in a highlight film while B will score more. Personally, I've always preferred substance over style but the choice is yours.

Don't be fooled into thinking that Mark Roth, Pete Weber, or Amleto Monacelli owe all of their success to power. All three possess outstanding control. In fact, Amleto's ascendancy to becoming a truly exceptional pro dates to when he acquired the ability to hit his target more consistently.

The keys to remember when it comes to greater striking power are:

**1.** Hit the proper pocket with sufficient power and at the correct angle to set off the desired chain reaction.

**2.** Maintain enough speed to avoid deflection but do not fling a Nolan Ryan–like fastball.

**3.** Save the nose hits for fighters and try to travel to Brooklyn as little as possible.

**4.** If you executed a good delivery but went high or light (or missed the pocket entirely), make an adjustment.

**5.** Don't fall in love with the huge hook ball. Instead combine power with accuracy.

**6.** Learn how to get the edge on your opponent with your knowledge and your decision-making ability. You can make up for a lot of shortcomings with superior concentration and strategy.

There is one other factor that is crucial. You can't become overly upset when you've been "robbed." It's a fact of bowling life that the player who hits the pocket the most also figures to be tapped more than someone who is all over the place.

This sport can be enormously frustrating, especially when a long string of strikes is halted by a pin that had no right to remain standing. On my level, one unfortunate 9 pin sandwiched by a series of strikes deducts 21 sticks from my final score. Very often that can determine the difference between winning or losing a match.

It is upsetting, but you must avoid getting upset. Keep an even keel, secure in the knowledge that luck tends to even out over the course of time. If you get angry you will only lose your concentration on the task at hand. Believe me, bowling is a tough enough challenge without making it more difficult for yourself by losing your cool.

One final word. Today's equipment is designed to yield maximum performance benefits. Urethane balls, in trained hands, can work miracles. The pins just don't stand a chance.

Remind yourself that the reason you spent so much money on a bowling ball was so it can do most of the work for you. Avoid the temptation to overthrow. Be smooth, use a controlled hook, hit your target, and observe your shots carefully. Do all of these things right and *X will* mark the spot!

# 5
# Simple Spare Conversions

While it's true that stringing strikes wins games, your ability to cover the basic spares will help you to avoid losing matches that you should win. There's nothing like a needless open frame to take the wind out of your sails and rejuvenate an opponent who thought he or she was beaten.

Reputation counts for a lot in bowling, especially when you reach the level where you are competing seriously. I have won a lot of matches that I probably deserved to lose in local tournaments simply because my rival fell apart after taking a lead. I could almost see him thinking, "Wow, I'm beating a Touring pro."

Part of that aura was a perception on his part that I would come through in the clutch. I've found that if my opponent thinks that I won't beat myself, he is more likely to panic and come unraveled when I take the lead.

On the other hand, if you should develop a reputation as someone who misses easy spares you will allow your opponents to maintain confidence even when they're behind. One of the biggest differences between bowling's top Touring pros and the pack is that the best players don't donate games by failing to cover the basic spare conversion attempts.

The secret to spare shooting involves a combination of accuracy, knowing basic strategies, and being a fundamentally sound player. If you take my advice to heart and develop a straight armswing coupled with consistent timing, you should have little difficulty when faced with most spare leaves.

I strongly recommend that all of your movements be directed toward your target. Some players walk to the left when making a left-to-right shot (or vice versa). There are even Touring pros with crossover footwork that takes them away from their target during their deliveries. These unnecessary complications are, in my opinion, counterproductive.

I make it a point to walk directly at my target. If you drew a line from my arm it would dissect my target arrow and end up on the pin at which I am aiming.

Almost all of the PBA and LPBT Tours' better spare shooters are players who avoid superfluous motions. Their movements are simple and fall into the parallel-perpendicular categories that I described earlier.

It's also no coincidence that the PBA Tour's greatest stars are outstanding spare shooters. While Mark Roth, Marshall Holman, Brian Voss, Mike Aulby, Pete Weber, Dave Husted, Dave Ferraro, Parker Bohn III, Amleto Monacelli, Walter Ray Williams, Jr., Joe Berardi, Mark Williams, Tony Westlake, and Del Ballard, Jr.—to name a few—all feature excellent strike balls, they are equally proficient on their second shots.

The same holds true on the women's Tour. I have been extremely impressed with the shot-making skills of Lorrie Nichols, Robin Romeo, and other LPBT stars after competing with them in mixed doubles events in recent years.

An inability to make spares can retard a player's progress. The pro ranks have scores of young prospects who are discovering the hard way that all the revs in the world for great strike shot carry won't count for much if every four-

*Marshall Holman ranks among the sport's most outstanding spare shooters.* Courtesy Professional Bowlers Association

bagger is negated with an open frame. Power players like Monacelli and Mark Baker vastly improved themselves after upgrading their spare games.

They learned to cut down their hook to become more accurate. In 1989 Amleto was second on the Tour in average, cashed in 22 of 28 events, and paced all PBA pros with 10 match play appearances. He won four tournaments and became only the third pro to top the $200,000 plateau in a single year by winning $213,815.

In 1990 he became the second professional bowler to top $200,000 twice (Mike Aulby was the first). For good measure, Amleto joined Earl Anthony, Mark Roth, and Don Johnson as the only men in PBA history to have been honored Player of the Year in consecutive years.

That's a far cry from what Monacelli was able to accomplish in his first few years as a pro. It wasn't until his sixth year on Tour that he won his first tournament. His emergence as one of the PBA's dominant players coincides with a greatly improved all-around game. Prior to that, he could strike with any foe but he gave away many matches by squandering simple conversions.

Spare shooting is—and should be—a relatively easy proposition. While rolling a strike requires a combination of accuracy *and* power, covering all but a handful of the trickiest leaves is simply a matter of hitting your target. All of the single-pin spares are a piece of cake.

I am always amazed at how many medium- to high-average bowlers (who ought to know better) hook their ball at single-pin leaves. You do not need any power whatsoever to knock over a three-and-a-half pound pin with a bowling ball. And putting 15 revs on your shot won't be of any use if you miss the pin.

## THE SHORTEST DISTANCE BETWEEN TWO POINTS IS . . .

. . . a straight line.

When shooting a spare that involves double wood (e.g., any cluster that includes one or more of the following combinations: the 2-8, 1-5, or 3-9), power is required. In those cases, you can't afford to have your ball deflect after impacting against the front pin or the back stick may be left standing.

However, on all spares *not* involving double wood, power is superfluous. All that counts is accuracy.

The easiest way to maintain consistency is to roll a modest hook on your strike shots so that little or no adjustment with your delivery mechanics is required when shooting spares and splits. The next best approach is to learn how to kill the curvature on your spare attempts if you are someone who uses a big hook on your strike shots.

There are four popular kill options. The first involves using different equipment. A hard-shell ball—especially balls made of rubber—tends to hook very little. Using a straight-type ball for most spare and split leaves will allow you to avoid having to make a major change in how you release your shot.

Beware, however, that your bowling ball's characteristics will be altered with use. The next time you visit the lanes, check out the track area of your ball. You'll notice a lot of wear and tear with the various nicks resembling a tire's tread pattern.

The greater the wear and tear on the track area of your ball, the more friction will be created between it and the lane. That in turn will make it hook more after it leaves the oily (front) section and enters the dry part (the back end) of the alley.

To keep the surface of your ball from excessively gripping the lane, use the Lustre King machine that's found in virtually every bowling center. It will polish your ball to give its surface a high gloss. Invest a quarter (or two) on a regular basis and you will greatly help your straight spare ball to continue to go as straight as possible.

The drawback to changing equipment for your spare conversions is that no two balls will have exactly the same feel. No matter how much expertise your ball driller might possess, the grips and holes of your strike and spare balls won't be identical. Some individuals find this to be disconcerting.

An alternative is to either keep your wrist straight (to modify your hook if you don't naturally cover a lot of boards) or, if you throw a big hook ball, "break" your wrist backwards throughout your delivery. Although this will feel awkward at first, it is an effective way of keeping your shot straight.

So, too, with the so-called suitcase grip. Hold the ball as if it were the handle of a suitcase with your thumb on the inside and your fingers on the outside. The latter are around the 3 o'clock (for a righty) or the 9 o'clock position (for a lefty). Maintain that grip throughout your armswing and follow-through.

*The normal strike shot release (left) can be altered. Dave uses the so-called suitcase grip (right) to help to kill his shot's hook.* Dan Chidester

Whatever occurs, do *not* impart any lift or rotate your hand during your release. Sounds tricky? It is. That's why the skill of killing a shot is one that is best learned by taking a lesson from a reputable pro.

Finally, you can add ball speed. The faster your shot, the less it will hook. Just be careful not to throw the ball so hard that you lose accuracy by being off balance.

By adding speed coupled with killing your release, your ball will go even straighter. The spare formula on the PBA and LPBT Tours is simple: the fewer boards your ball covers, the more spares and splits that you will convert.

Regardless of how many of these four options you

decide to incorporate into your game, being fundamentally sound is key. Players with armswings that are all over the place, who open their shoulder or flip-flop their wrist or hand positions during their delivery will not fill a lot of frames.

Just by doing the little things right you should be able to make almost all of your spares. You can become a very good bowler without a great strike ball, especially with today's equipment, which will supply much of the carry power for you. Without rolling a single strike it is still possible to produce a 190 game.

Some spares require little change from your strike line. Covering a 5 pin involves the exact same approach as you used on the previous ball. That's why it's considered so easy that bowlers love to kid each other that "nobody misses the 5 pin."

Having said that, I still say you should never lose concentration when faced with an easy spare. The turning point when I beat Amleto Monacelli in the title game of the 1991 Firestone Tournament of Champions came when he missed the 5 pin. Imagine that—the man who is arguably the world's premiere player missed the easiest of spares. If Amleto can miss it, so can the rest of us. Never take anything for granted, even if it's a spare you should cover every time.

In reality, all single-pin leaves (except for the corner pins) are only marginally more difficult than the 5. Even the 7 pin and the 10 pin shouldn't intimidate you if you use the right strategy and are a fundamentally sound player.

The bowler who directs all movements at the target should have little problem as long as you don't allow yourself to be distracted or unnerved by the proximity of the gutter.

## THE CROSS-LANE STRATEGY

With a single-pin leave your key is to roll the ball directly at your target. The next most important factor is where you stand. On any leave in which neither the headpin nor the 5 pin is standing, draw an imaginary line from the headpin

*Crosslane >*
*Strategy*

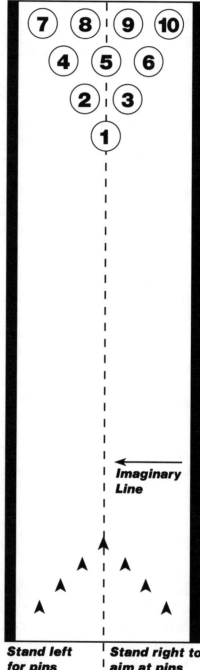

Stand left
for pins
3, 6, 9, & 10

Stand right to
aim at pins
2, 4, 7, & 8

through the fourth (center) arrow to the settee area. Always stand on the *opposite* side of the approach from your target pin (see accompanying diagram).

I'm amazed how many bowlers will shoot a 10 pin by standing all the way to the right side of the lane and rolling their ball just inside of the gutter. Their margin for error is slight. They minimize the amount of lane surface at their disposal.

The cross-lane strategy gives you a far better angle, especially when shooting at corner pins. Never attempt to convert a 7 or a 10 pin by rolling the ball right alongside the gutter. I can't think of a single pro bowler—or even one of the better amateurs—who deviates from this basic principle.

## LINING UP ON THE APPROACH: THE THIRD ARROW METHOD

One spare-shooting method is to always use the third arrow as your target. Which board you will stand on will depend on what pin remains. To use this technique will require some experimentation on your part.

Start by attempting a 2 pin if you're right-handed or a 3 pin if you are a lefty. With the third arrow as your target, place your sliding foot on about the 15th board. Roll the ball straight and hit that target.

Make slight side-to-side adjustments in your starting position until you find that a ball rolled over your target impacts against the middle of the object pin. When that occurs, make a mental note of where you stood on the approach for future reference.

It is very important that you commit to memory the numbers of each board. Remember that the first board is the one next to the gutter that's on the same side as your bowling hand. The 39th board is found next to the opposite gutter (the left channel for right-handed players or the right channel for left-handers).

Remember too that the arrows are five boards apart. The first arrow is found on the fifth board with the second arrow on the 10th board and so on. If someone told you that his or her aiming point was the 12th board, you'd instantly recognize that spot as being between the second and third arrows.

Through trial and error you have gained a reference point for all other single-pin spare conversion attempts. As you can see from the accompanying diagram, I have assigned the pins various letters. The reference pin we just discussed is defined as pin C. For every letter change you should move approximately three boards (you will discover how many based on more trial and error).

Move in the direction of your bowling hand for an A or a B cover. Move toward your sliding foot to shoot any of the pins that are labeled E, F, or G.

As noted before, the headpin and the 5 pin are treated like a strike ball. Stand on your strike spot while using the same arrow that you do when all 10 pins are standing.

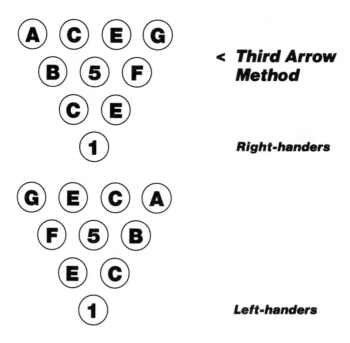

**< Third Arrow Method**

**Right-handers**

**Left-handers**

## THE PROS' FORMULA

OK, class, it's time for more visualization exercises. Let's imagine a bowling lane. Using the cross-lane strategy, right-handed players should draw an imaginary line from the 3 pin through a target arrow (either the third or fourth arrow is recommended). Continue that line through the back of the approach.

You southpaws should do the same, using the 2 pin as your starting point.

You can do this either on a piece of paper or by standing on the approach. If you do it while standing on the approach, keep in mind that your eyes are not aligned with your bowling hand. To compensate, move your target two boards to the right (if you are a right-handed player) or to the left (left-handed bowlers). Or you can keep the same target and simply move your feet one board to the left (right-handers) or the right (for you lefties).

Where your imaginary line ends is the approximate spot where you should stand for shooting cross-lane *if* you're capable of throwing the ball perfectly straight. If your shots hook slightly, start a little bit deeper on the approach by standing more toward the opposite side from your bowling hand (righties move left).

For covering the next pin over (the 6 pin for a right-hander or the 4 pin for a left-hander) move three boards deeper while maintaining the same target. To convert a corner pin (the 10 pin for righties, the 7 pin for lefties) move an additional three boards deeper for a total of a six-board move from your original position.

You can do the same on the opposite side of the lane. Right-handed bowlers begin with a 2-pin cover while left-ies start at the 3 pin. This time, move three boards outside to shoot the next pin over (the 4 pin for righties, the 6 pin for lefties) and a total of six boards for the corner pin (the 7 pin for righties and the 10 pin for lefties).

## MAKING SPARES OFF YOUR STRIKE LINE

Also known as the 3-6-10 formula, this is another adjustment strategy that's popular on both pro circuits. It can be
employed any time that your strike line involves the second, third, fourth, or fifth arrow as your target. However, it
cannot be used when the first arrow provides your strike
shot target.

Let's say you've left the 5 pin. That means your strike
shot was light. Move one board toward the side of your
bowling hand. Use your strike shot target. Your ball should
impact on the center of the 5 pin.

As you can see, the accompanying diagram lists the 5
pin as A. The pins that are five boards removed from it are
listed as B. These are the 2, 3, 8, and 9 pins. The ones that
are 10 boards from the center of the lane are assigned the
letter C. These are the 4 and 6 pins. Finally, the corner pins
are in the D category.

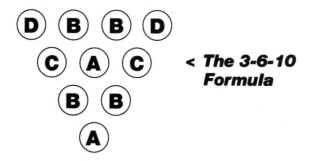

*< The 3-6-10
Formula*

For every letter, a three-board move is involved. Thus,
to shoot one of the C pins involves a six-board adjustment
from your 5-pin line. If the C pin that you are attempting to
convert is the one on the right side (the 6 pin), move to the
left. If it's on the left side of the lane (the 4 pin), move your
feet six boards to the right. Simple, isn't it?

Consider these formulas as bowling's equivalent of
buying a pair of pants. After you find the one that fits your
style the best, it may still be necessary to have it altered.

Tailor your game through modest changes that result from your trial-and-error experimentation.

Let's say you fail to cover a 10 pin because your ball sails where the 6 pin is normally placed. You've missed the center of the 10 pin by five boards. For every two boards that you missed you should move your target one board in the opposite direction. In this case, your ball went five boards to the left of where you had hoped. To compensate, move your target two and a half boards to the right.

You can also keep the target but move your feet one board for every two that you missed. Many players feel more comfortable moving their feet so they can always use an arrow as their focal point.

## AN ALTERNATE STRATEGY FOR LINING UP YOUR CONVERSION ATTEMPTS

I have written the following spare cover descriptions for the majority of bowlers who are right-handed players. Those of you who are left-handed should translate by putting everything in a mirror. Thus, my advice on shooting a 10 pin is applicable to your efforts to cover a 7 pin. When I say to move right, you move to the left.

Let's start with what many players regard as their number one enemy, the 10 pin. Of all the common situations in bowling, none is so falsely intimidating. Judging by the attitude that far too many players bring to this shot, one would think that the right channel is the kegling equivalent of shark-infested water through which you must swim.

Instead of being concerned with your ball falling into that deep blue sea, concentrate solely on your target. I find the third or the fourth (center) arrow to be my favorite aiming points. If it were up to me, I'd stand as far left on the approach as possible while looking at the fourth arrow. Doing so gives me the greatest cross-lane advantage.

In some centers, that's not always possible on the right-hand lane due to the ball-return apparatus obstructing access. I might move a few boards to the right with my stance while moving my target to the third arrow.

*A protrusive ball-return apparatus, such as at Fairlawn's (Ohio) famed Riviera Lanes, can affect your starting position.* Russ Vitale

Just convince yourself that all you need to do to make this spare is roll your ball smoothly but without any appreciable degree of hook over that arrow. Remember, you need to use as much speed as you are capable of generating without compromising your balance or timing. Now that's not so hard, is it?

The more you naturally hook your shot, the more important it is that you add speed. Naturally straight Tour shooters like Dave Ferraro and Walter Ray Williams, Jr., don't need to throw the ball hard to keep it on line. In contrast, Mark Roth and Joe Berardi go with a fast ball on their single-pin spare covers.

Lane conditions also dictate whether it's vital to make a concerted effort at being straight by adding speed, changing equipment, or killing your release.

If this were gymnastics, your score would be multiplied by a degree of difficulty determined by the amount of oil on the lane. If the alley is very dry, the tendency of your ball to hook more will create accuracy problems.

On most house conditions you should be able to execute a natural release unless you are an ultra-power player.

The 6 is slightly easier than the 10 pin because there is some room for your shot to hook back after you have let the ball out to the right. The physical steps necessary for a conversion aren't any different from what you must do to make a 10-pin conversion (or any other single-pin leave, for that matter).

I suggest moving your feet about three boards to the right of where you had lined up to cover the 10 pin. Once again, use your favorite target (I use the third or fourth arrow). As always, stay down with your shot until your follow-through has been completed and you have seen your ball roll through the arrows.

Move another three boards to the right from where you shot the 6 pin to cover the 3 pin. Maintain the same target and be certain to execute the proper fundamentals we've already covered in this chapter.

To make the 3-6 combination, split the difference between the two moves. I stand four to five boards right of where I would have for a 10 pin.

Some people play their strike ball line for this spare. Since you probably just went high (or slightly Brooklyn) on your first ball and since you want your shot to impact against the right side of the pin, move your feet two to three boards to the left of where you normally stand on your strike shot. Either method should work well for you.

Shooting off your strike line requires using the same release, speed, and equipment for your second ball. That's not such a hot strategy if you're a player who covers a lot of boards. It is possible to use your strike line while killing a shot with more speed and a harder shell, but I couldn't begin to guess how many boards you'll need to adjust. That's something only you big hook bowlers can discover for yourselves by taking a lot of notes on your trial-and-error experimentation.

Left-sided spares can be a tricky proposition on lanes with uneven oil patterns. When covering a right-sided spare, you are going against the grain of the wood. This also helps to inhibit a shot's hook.

Your cross-lane strategy for left-sided pins means that you will now be going up the boards. Your ball will hook earlier if the lane is extremely dry. Fortunately, in most houses there is dependable oil in the middle of a lane. That's because with rare exceptions the center section gets the least amount of play, so it retains the most oil (because oil evaporation and movement are caused by the friction of bowling balls).

The only surefire way of knowing the oil distribution is to use your warm-up period to shoot at least one cross-lane spare on each side of the lane. You don't want any surprises when a miss could prove costly.

Remember, more oil means less hook while a dry lane makes for more hook. If you are in the (bad!) habit of covering a lot of boards by throwing a big hook at single-pin leaves, you may pay a big price when it comes time to go left to right to cover what should be a relatively easy spare.

A player who goes dead straight at spares hardly has to be as concerned with lane conditions. Even given the less predictable aspect of rolling up the boards to the Brooklyn side, the player who uses less hook has eliminated most of his or her guesswork.

That's not to say that lane conditioner won't be at least a minor factor. I know of some straight-shot players whose ball will actually back up on heavy oil. That has happened to me on occasion. By knowing your game and the condi-

tions on which you are competing, you can make adjustments to compensate for such factors.

Whether the alley is almost as dry as the Sahara Desert
or nearly as oily as pit row at the Indy 500 won't affect you
so much if you make the equipment/speed/release adjustments we've covered. Your ball will go relatively straight no
matter what.

Not so with the big hook player. That type of bowler
must guess at how his or her shot will react. That player
could do everything right—from executing a good delivery
to hitting the target—only to discover an unexpected oil
splotch that causes him or her to miss to the right or a dry
area has induced the ball to take off well to the left of the
pin.

As for me, in such a spot I line up so my ball will hit
just to the near (right) side of the pin. My ball hooks very
slightly. As always, I employ the cross-lane strategy. I am
careful not to rear up. Instead, I stay down with my shot
and execute a good knee bend and follow-through at my
target.

Be careful that all of your movements are directed at
your target. There are exceptions. Some big hookers walk
to the left, open their shoulders, and then throw the ball
back to their right in the hope that it will hook back toward
the pins. That is far more complicated than my approach.
That's another reason that keeping things simple is best,
especially if you can't roll 100+ practice games per week.

Having left the 2 pin, I know that my strike shot was
light. I move one board to the right to compensate for that
and another three boards because the 2 pin is five boards
left of center. I add three boards' worth of adjustment for
every subsequent pin (thus, a seven-board move for the 4
pin and a 10-board move for the 7 pin).

If the lane is very dry, I might only move two boards to
my right for the 2 pin. If so, then I'll move five boards for
the 4 pin (a three-board adjustment added to the initial
two-board move) and eight boards for the 7 pin.

Under no circumstances should you ever *belly* your

shot at a left-sided spare (unless it involves double wood). In plain English, don't aim for a lower-numbered board than the one on which you are standing. The ball's break point—especially when initiated against the grain of the wood—is hard to predict. You will never see me standing on the 30th board and aiming for the third arrow (15th board) to shoot a left-sided spare.

That's because I have witnessed so many needless failures by players who do so. There is no sense in projecting your shot left to right for a left-sided spare. It subjects you to the whims of invisible (and almost impossible to detect) oil patterns.

Keep in mind that all of the options with starting positions and targets I have mentioned are what work for most players. You may naturally hook the ball a bit more or less than the norm. Or the center in which you bowl has certain quirks to which you must adjust. Only through trial and error will you discover the spare-shooting formulas that work best for you.

No matter what, always roll the ball as straight as possible with all of your movements directed toward your target. Doing the little things right pays big dividends when covering single-pin spares.

Perhaps the most significant common denominator among the best spare shooters is their attitude. They recognize the importance of filling frames and work just as hard in practice on their spare games as they do at improving their strike shot.

Walter Ray Williams, Jr., and Dave Ferraro—talented though they are—do not rank high among contemporary pros when it comes to carrying power. But both have been dominant players for a considerable period of time because they are so fundamentally sound. It's exceedingly rare when they beat themselves in a match by failing to cover their spares. It's an often overlooked part of the game in which I take a lot of pride. You should, too.

# 6
# Spare Cluster and Split Conversions

There are two basic varieties of multiple-pin spare conversions: those that involve double wood and those that don't. A double-wood spare occurs when a cluster of pins includes either the 2-8 or the 3-9 combination. A third possibility, but one that occurs about as infrequently as a solar eclipse, is the 1-5 combo.

The presence of the sleeper (back) pin means that your shot must be both accurate and powerful for your ball to impact against both sticks. To accomplish that, your shot should contact anywhere from the center of the front pin to its near side.

A right-handed player's ball that is hooking from right to left can hit to the right side of center of the pin and still do the job. For that to occur, however, you must avoid excess deflection, which is why sufficient inertia and power must be imparted.

Double-wood spares are the most difficult nonsplit that you will face. I'm sure that if you polled the pros you would find that the 3-6-9-10 (for the right-handers) or the 2-4-7-8 (lefties) would be rated as the least favorite spare.

*Like all the top pros, David applies just as much concentration to his spare and split conversions as he does to his strike shots.* Russ Vitale

The next toughest is the so-called bucket (the 2-4-5-8 for the right-handed players or the 3-5-6-9 for left-handed bowlers).

Both of these types of double-wood spares require power and accuracy. The shot must be rolled over a seldom-used part of the lane. An added dilemma is the possible surprise that could arise from either an unexpected excess or a dearth of oil.

Other types of spares present different challenges. Most power players aren't very fond of multiple-pin leaves in which the front stick is to the Brooklyn side of the back one. Right-handers don't like it when that front pin is to the left of the back pin while left-handers aren't fond of seeing the front pin to the right of the back stick.

Among the spares in this category that we right-handed players could live without are the 2-5, 5-9, 3-6, and the 3-6-10, to name a few. Their equivalent for left-handed bowlers are the 3-5, 5-8, 2-4, and the 2-4-7.

To convert these, your shot should be aimed at the near side of the lower (or lowest) numbered pin. The ball will hit both pins. In the case of the 3-6-10 or the 2-4-7 it will send the second pin into the highest-numbered stick. You will also make your spare if your ball crosses over to the Brooklyn side of the lower- (lowest-) numbered pin to send it into the other stick(s).

What adds a degree of difficulty is that all of the above are easily "chopped." A chop occurs when your ball breaks so sharply at the back end that it hits just to the near side of the center of the front pin. When that happens neither the ball nor the target pin deflects to take out the back stick.

One strategy for avoiding a chop for the right-handed player is to stand on the left side of the approach and to roll your ball from left to right. Southpaws do the opposite, moving to the far right side of the lane to execute a right-to-left trajectory.

Personally, I find it easier to kill my shot while playing roughly the same line as I would to aim at the lower-number pin as if it were the only pin standing. To guard against a chop I will move my feet a board or two to the left (left-handed bowlers move right).

For example, a right-handed player faced with the 2-5 will use the same target as if only the 2 pin were standing. Now move your feet slightly (one or, at most, two boards) left of where you would normally position yourself for a 2 pin conversion. The left-handed player attempting to convert the 3-5 uses the 3-pin target while moving slightly to the right on the approach.

## SHOOTING THE BUCKET

The bucket (2-4-5-8/3-5-6-9) presents us with the worst of both worlds. A high hit can result in a chop in which the 5 pin remains. A light or a Brooklyn hit on a hook shot makes it unlikely that you will knock over that pesky back pin.

There are two schools of thought among Touring pros. The majority of us hook the ball into the pocket (the 2-5 or the 3-5, depending on the hand you use). A minority of pros prefer to shoot hard and straight down the opposite side of the lane. PBA Hall of Fame member Joe Berardi, who ranks among the best spare shooters on the Tour, is a right-handed player who stands on the far left side of the lane to make the bucket. So does Marc McDowell.

Their theory is that you need only to be accurate using that strategy whereas the rest of us need accuracy *and* power. The disadvantage to this approach is that the added speed they use makes accuracy harder to obtain for most of us. In some cases that's not a detriment, because Joe and

**To convert the bucket, the right-handed player places the shot into the 2-5 zone, with the ball's hooking momentum helping to carry it into the 8 pin.** Dan Chidester

Marc have a great ability to throw hard without sacrificing accuracy.

To use the Berardi method, move your feet to around the 35th to 39th board so that you will release your shot with your sliding foot just inside the opposite gutter. Through trial and error you will learn where to stand while using the sixth arrow (which is the second one in from the far side) as your target.

They aim to hit the middle of the front pin. If the ball impacts on the Brooklyn portion of that stick it's as if they were making the 2-5 and the 4-8 spares. Instead of their ball driving through to eliminate the back pin, the 4 pin does the work.

As for the rest of us who use the more conventional strategy, we use the same target as our strike ball while moving our feet three to five boards in the direction of our bowling hand (to the right for right-handers, to the left for left-handers).

By shooting the bucket off our strike line, we use a portion of the lane with which we are familiar while making the most minimal adjustments from our first shot.

In contrast to Joe Berardi, I have always felt more comfortable by staying on my normal side of the approach. But remember that the one rule of bowling is that what counts is how many. If you aren't successful using the conventional strategy, give Joe's way a try to see what works better for you.

## THE 2-4-5/3-5-6

The elimination of the back pin from the bucket means that you now need only accuracy, not power. Your biggest enemy is the possibility of the chop. Make an added effort to throw a straight ball, either with an equipment change or by killing the hook. Remember, a kill shot is accomplished by using the suitcase grip described previously or by adding ball speed, changing equipment, bending your wrist backward, or any combination of these.

Another tactic: a righty moves one or two boards left

from where he or she would shoot the 2 pin. A lefty moves one or two boards to the right from where he or she would stand for the 3 pin.

The Berardi/McDowell bucket angle also works. I would urge caution before employing that strategy if you have a tendency to pull your shots, you roll even a slight hook, or you suspect that there may be a big difference in the amount of conditioner between the left and right sides of the alley.

The latter could be the case when freshly applied conditioner has become dispersed by a series of shots. Carrydown changes the characteristics of the part of the lane that has gotten the most usage.

## THE PICKET FENCE

You have missed the headpin entirely and your punishment is to face either the 1-2-4-7 or the 1-3-6-10. Before tossing your second ball you should ascertain what you did wrong on your first shot so as not to repeat that mistake. That's especially important for this spare as you will attempt to roll your shot the same as you would your strike ball.

You roll your normal first shot when the picket fence is on the same side of the lane as your bowling hand. Should it be on the opposite flank, keep your strike shot target while moving your feet three boards. Right-handed bowlers move to the right; left-handed players stand farther left on the approach. Either way, you must execute a good shot.

The tougher of the two picket fences is the 1-3-6-10 for a right-handed player and the 1-2-4-7 for a lefty. Even though there isn't any double wood, you need to produce sufficient power to avoid deflection. If you fail to do so, you will be left with a soft 10 (righties) or the soft 7 (lefties). Making a picket fence that's on the far side (1-3-6-10 for lefties; 1-2-4-7 for the rest of us) involves having your ball impact on the Brooklyn side of the headpin.

You can also make the opposite-sided fence with your normal strike ball, but that's risky. A light hit will leave the

2 pin (for right-handed players) or the 3 pin (lefties) up-right. A high hit likely will fail to topple the 4 pin (righties) or the 6 pin (lefties). Even a seemingly good shot sometimes sees the 7 pin (righties) or the 10 pin (lefties) refuse to fall. That's why if the picket fence is on the Brooklyn side of the lane, your ball should travel there too.

## THE 1-2-4/1-3-6
This is the picket fence minus that corner pin. The same strategies apply, although there is a bit more margin for error. Once again, if the pins are on the far side of the lane you should move your feet a few boards toward your bowling hand to have your shot cross over to the Brooklyn side.

## THE WASHOUT
The dreaded washout occurs when the headpin and one of the corner pins are upright with the pins between them eliminated. Not only are you called upon to execute a shot

*Here's how to carry the washout, in this case to make the 1-2-4-10 combination.* Dan Chidester

on which pinpoint control is vital, you have to do it after rolling such a poor strike ball that you missed the headpin entirely.

The presence of the headpin means this isn't officially categorized as a split. Nevertheless, it's more difficult than many types of split leaves.

In most cases, the corner pin will be the one on the side of your bowling hand. It will often be joined by at least a part of the picket fence on the Brooklyn side of the headpin. Right-handed bowlers will most often face the 1-10, 1-2-10, and the 1-2-4-10. Lefties are usually challenged by the 1-7, 1-3-7, and the 1-3-6-7.

The object is to aim as if you were trying to produce a Brooklyn strike. The ball will take out the headpin and all of its companions on the opposite side. If all goes as planned, the headpin will slide into the corner stick.

I use the same target as on my strike ball while moving my feet two to three boards to the side of my bowling hand. One danger to avoid is having the headpin fly around the neck of the corner pin. If you are someone who throws the ball exceptionally fast you may have to decrease your shot's speed.

Unless you roll a straight ball, the loss of velocity will mean more hooking action. You might wish to either modify the number of boards that you move with your feet or perhaps even line up on the same spot as you would for a strike ball. The bigger the hook you normally roll, the greater number of added boards your shot will cover when propelled with less speed. You should move your feet less (if at all) compared to those who feature less hook.

## THE 3-6-10/2-4-7

Having gone through the nose on your first ball, you are now faced with the 3-6-10 (right-handers) or the 2-4-7 (southpaws).

Aim your ball so it goes between the two lower-numbered pins. The cross-lane strategy works best here. My feet are two boards to the right from where I would stand for the 6-pin leave. You left-handed bowlers will move the same distance to the left from where you would shoot a 4 pin.

If all goes as planned, my ball will take out the 3 pin and the 6 pin with the 6 pin deflecting into the 10. A mirror imagine of that chain reaction occurs for southpaws.

While some players use the hard-and-straight strategy while shooting cross-lane, I've always preferred to use a hook ball. Through experience I've learned that at the back end the boards nearest the gutters are almost always dry.

I stand at such a spot on the left side of the approach so that my ball will get within a few boards of the right gutter before it begins to hook. There's usually enough oil in the middle of the lane to provide a "hold" area should I tug (pull) my shot to the left.

Some ultra-power players find that they can't move their feet far enough cross-lane to accommodate their huge hook. Only if you fall into that category would I recommend using a kill shot.

As with all spare and split formulas, you will need to experiment to discover what best suits your game. A good starting point might be to stand around the 35th board while aiming for the third arrow. Through trial and error you can adjust your feet depending on how much your ball hooks (big hook players must stand farther cross-lane than straight shooters).

## THE 3-6-9-10/2-4-7-8

The addition of the 9 pin (righties) or the 8 pin (lefties) greatly increases the degree of difficulty. Double wood calls for a combination of power and accuracy. That's the reason that this is the spare most feared on the pro Tours.

What makes it extra difficult is that you need to generate virtually as much power as you would to roll a strike, but your pocket has moved five boards toward the near-sided gutter. There isn't very much room to let your ball out. This presents a problem for the big hook bowler. The relatively straight shooter who lacks sufficient revs for great power must have pinpoint accuracy to carry the back pin.

As with all double-wood spares, my equipment choice is to use my normal strike ball. My feet are deep inside, usually in the neighborhood of the 37th board, with the third arrow as my target. As for your game, adjust your starting point based on your needs.

When playing on a lane in which my strike line is to play the gutter, I might adjust my target for this spare to the second arrow. Either way, I want my ball to continue to move away from the target pin after my shot has passed through the arrows. I've found that the ideal break point (where my shot begins to hook) is found between the second and the fourth boards.

The exception to this strategy occurs on those very rare occasions on the Pro Tour in which the lane maintenance crew has put up an "out of bounds." As in golf, that's a spot on the lane from which recovery is impossible should your shot stray. In bowling, that's accomplished by putting down extra oil on the boards nearest to the gutter. Hit those and your ball is virtually guaranteed to disappear into the channel.

When faced with that, I will throw hard and straight while aiming a little left of the 3 pin. I find that my ball will actually back up into the target. The subsequent deflection after impacting against the 3 pin guarantees a conversion.

Although it's almost assured that you will never face a condition that features an OB (out of bounds), you might wish to give this alternative strategy a try if you don't have any luck with the more conventional approach.

## AN OVERVIEW

We have now covered the more common spare cluster leaves. Perhaps the best advice I can offer on how to avoid missing them is what my coaches told me as I was growing up. "Just don't leave them," they would say.

Although that strategy is meant to be tongue-in-cheek, there is much truth in their advice. The tougher cluster combinations result from rolling a very poor strike ball. That makes the conversion all the more difficult, because your confidence has likely suffered somewhat from failing to execute properly on your preceding shot.

Your two ways to avoid missing the bucket, the picket fence, the washout, and the like are to follow the strategy I have outlined coupled with ample practice—or to listen to my coaches. Given my choice of those two options, I would definitely endorse the latter.

## THE MOST COMMON SPLITS AND HOW TO MAKE THEM

With the exception of the baby split (3-10/2-7), the odds are less than 50-50 for even a pro bowler to convert the other varieties of splits. Ironically, that is precisely the reason that you should practice them. There's nothing quite like averting a seemingly certain open with a spectacularly successful split conversion to elevate your spirits while deflating those of your opponents.

With practice, you should make your share of splits. For example, the 5-7 (for right-handed bowlers) and the 5-10 (for lefties) aren't nearly as difficult as they seem. All you need to do is throw the equivalent of a very light strike ball to slide the 5 pin into that corner stick. Your adjustment is to roll your ball over your strike shot target while moving your feet two boards deeper on the approach (righties move left and vice versa).

The baby split is no different than the 3-6-10 (for righties) or the 2-4-7 (lefties). Just go cross-lane and hit to the far side of the lowest-numbered pin. As with a single pin leave, power isn't needed. In fact, the last thing you want to do is have your ball drive through the front pin. The idea is for your ball to deflect into the corner stick.

Because your ball is going across the grain of the wood your shot will be killed naturally unless you are an ultra-power player. Only if you have a huge hook should you make a concerted effort to kill your shot.

When two adjacent pins in the same row are upright a split is recorded although, as with the baby split, your ball can touch both pins: the 4-5, 5-6, 7-8, and 9-10 for example.

Attempt to fit your shot precisely between the two sticks. If you have the 9-10 you use your 10-point target while moving your feet a board or two to the right. That tactic works for both left- and right-handed bowlers.

A good way to remember your strategy is to use the target of the higher-numbered pin coupled with a one- or two-board move of your feet to your right. Or, if that isn't to your liking, use the target for the lower-numbered pin accompanied by a one- or two-board move to the left.

The most difficult of the so-called makable splits are the 4-7-10 and the 6-7-10. For the former, use your 7-pin target while moving your feet one board to the left. For the latter, use the 10-pin target while moving one board to your right. If all goes as planned, your ball will just nick the far side of the lowest-numbered pin, which will cause it to slide across the lane to take out the opposite corner pin.

Just slightly less challenging is the 4-9 (righties) or the 6-8 (lefties). I approach this as if I were trying to cover a 7 pin, while you southpaws think of this as a 10-point cover. Move one board away from the side of your bowling hand to give yourself a better angle. The hope is to hit the far side of the lower-numbered pin so that it will slide across the lane to knock over the back-row stick.

Most of the splits that we have discussed are difficult but not impossible. The bigger the gap between the pins, the more you have to weigh the consequences of attempting a conversion against the option of saving the wood. That becomes a key consideration in a close match when you are on a strike. Sometimes prudence beats valor. It's not always smart to go for the 4-7-10 and risk a gutter ball. Doing so while on a strike will cost you four certain pins on the scoresheet. It's up to you to bowl with your head as well as with your heart.

Having said that, there are certain splits that are viewed as "impossible" to convert. Any leave that involves pins in the same row that aren't adjacent falls in this category (the 7-10, 8-10, 7-9, 4-6, and the so-called big four— the 4-6-7-10). Also considered virtually unmakable is the

Greek Church. That's when you're faced with either the 4-6-7-8-10 or the 4-6-7-9-10.

Unless it's a desperation situation in which an open spells defeat, you are better advised to concede by going for the cluster with the greater number of pins. If there's an equal number on either side, aim for the half that's easier for you to cover.

If you are on a strike, the one pin that you knock over will count for two on the scoresheet. When your team makes it a policy to "save the wood" on all of your "unmakable" splits, sooner or later you will steal a close game from opponents who are careless.

It is possible to convert the 4-6, 7-9, or the 8-10 by barely touching the outside of one pin and sliding it into the other. This is a one-in-a-million shot although I have seen it done.

If you must attempt to convert these, your best odds are to throw a fastball worthy of Dave Stewart. Aim for the pin that's on the side closer to your bowling hand (right-handed bowlers shoot for the higher-numbered stick; left-handed players aim at the lower-numbered pin). Your hope is that your ball will hit the middle of that pin so that it is driven straight backward. Your ball collides a second time with the pin as they crash into the back wall with the pin ricocheting back into play.

A long shot? You bet. A fluke? Of course. But it can be done. As of 1990 the great Mark Roth was the only pro bowler to make the 7-10 on television. Roth—who has been honored after four seasons as the PBA's Bowler of the Year—accomplished that feat at the 1980 Alameda Open.

Then, in a period of a few months, Roth's feat was duplicated twice when John Mazza and Jess Stayrook both turned the trick.

I can name several top PBA stars, such as Dave Ferraro, who have told me that they have never converted any of the so-called unmakable splits. Because luck plays a far greater role than does skill, I'm almost always content merely to save the wood. I'm secure in the knowledge that my strat-

*Southpaws John Mazza and Jess Stayrook made the "impossible" 7-10 split during nationally televised title round competition just a few weeks apart.* Courtesy Professional Bowlers Association

egy of not donating pins will pay off in those games when the smallest of margins separates the winner from the loser.

As with covering most of your spare possibilities, being accurate is a far greater asset than being powerful. Just as with all aspects of bowling, being fundamentally sound will give you a great advantage. The thrill of making a difficult split in the 10th frame is just another incentive for you to work hard on keeping those shoulders square, walking toward your target, featuring a good pushaway, and having a straight armswing in which you disengage your muscles.

Get in the habit of doing those little things right and a lot of good big things will come your way!

# 7
# *Hooker's Paradise*

The one question that virtually every beginning and lower-average bowler loves to ask me is, "How do I make my ball hook?" It's as if that were the one great secret that will unlock the door to high scoring, as if you are somehow not a legitimate bowler until your shots take a circuitous route to the pocket.

Part of that perception has to do with role models. All pros and virtually every higher-average amateur rolls a hook ball. Learning to do so correctly will greatly improve your carry. Your shots will roll through the deck after contacting the headpin. Less deflection, as we already know, equals higher scoring.

There is a certain sex appeal to throwing a hook. Even after bowling tens of thousands of games I still get a special kick out of those times when the ball comes off of my hand just right and explodes into the pocket to clear the deck. It's a great feeling, bowling's equivalent of a slam dunk in basketball.

Having said that, I still say that not everyone is ready to throw a hook shot. Before attempting to add this weapon to your arsenal you should build a solid foundation based on good fundamental skills. I recommend attempting to learn the hook after you have achieved a reasonable consistency of motion during your delivery and have become fairly accurate.

As a general rule, you should be averaging at least 140 to 150 before scrapping that straight ball. When you were a baby you had to learn how to crawl before you could walk and you had to walk before you could run. Acquiring bowling skills is no different.

You will find the hook ball a lot easier to master if you have taken to heart my advice about the key physical components of good bowling. A quick review:

1. A good address position in which the ball is held in line with your bowling shoulder and your body is parallel (square) to the foul line.
2. On your pushaway you hand the ball forward and slightly upward so that gravity causes it to descend naturally.
3. A relaxed pendulum armswing that will be straight as an arrow if preceded by a proper pushaway. The elbow can be "flat" or you can slightly bend your arm.
4. Good timing so that your sliding foot arriving at the foul line is consistent with the release of your shot.
5. In most cases, maintaining the same wrist and hand position throughout your entire delivery (a brief disclaimer will follow).
6. A good knee bend by your sliding leg. Your sliding foot points either straight ahead or slightly inward (toward the side of your bowling hand).
7. Keep your eyes riveted on your target throughout your entire delivery.
8. A good follow-through at your target.

All of these ingredients are extremely helpful in developing a solid foundation upon which you may construct

***A pendulum armswing and good follow-through are two key ingredients in good bowling.*** Dan Chidester

the rest of your game. As with building a cathedral, the world's most magnificent steeple, stained glass windows, and stunning architecture won't count for much if the supporting structure collapses.

Likewise, that pretty hook ball of yours that explodes through the pins whenever it finds the pocket won't do much for your average if you aren't consistently accurate. No hook shot in the world—even if it had the combined power of Pete Weber and Amleto Monacelli—will overcome the pins if you fail to hit your target. Your first priority is to learn how to become consistently accurate. Once you can do that, you are ready to attempt the hook shot.

Now for that disclaimer that I promised.

The great majority of players—especially those of you whose practice time or natural skills are limited—do best when locking your wrist into one of the three basic positions throughout their entire delivery. There are, however, some who naturally do what is called wristing the ball. On the Tour this is also known as the load and unload technique.

Among its practitioners are some of bowling's top stars: Del Ballard, Jr., Marshall Holman, and Bob Benoit, to name a few. I can also do it when lane conditions merit, but I can't pretend to be anywhere near as proficient at it as the three gentlemen just named. They all do it naturally and on a regular basis.

When your wrist is cupped, the ball rolls down toward the palm of the hand during the downswing and the wrist position can actually change. It makes for a powerful strike ball when properly executed. The flip side is that it's far tougher to control, and the penalty for a bad shot is greater given that the sharper entry angle into the pins can make for some weird split combinations.

This is not a technique to learn from a book. A lesson from a pro could help, but even then, it's an approach best left to the pros and top-level amateurs.

Why do I mention it? Because there are a handful of amateurs to whom it comes naturally. It's similar to a neophyte golfer who can hit a drive 300 yards but whose shots don't always land in the fairway. I'm sure a golf pro wouldn't consider obtaining such distance to be a priority among the majority of players who have hit their drives in the 180–230 yard range. Having said that, I'm also sure that the same teaching pro wouldn't tell the 300-yard hitter to just hit it 210.

Don't change your game if wristing strike shots is something that you've been doing even without realizing it. But, unless that's the case, don't try learning this on your own, and then only after you've become a fundamentally sound player.

## THE PRINCIPLE BEHIND THE HOOK BALL

There are two major factors as to why a hook shot, when properly rolled, carries best.

First, the angle at which your ball approaches the pocket means that it is moving toward the middle of the rack rather than straight ahead. Even if a straight shot and a hook ball had the same amount of inertia and deflection, the angle of the hook's approach makes it the better candidate to drive through into the 5 pin.

Second, the hook ball's tracking pattern is superior. The majority of the ball's surface and weight is on the inside half of the ball, the part that's closer to the headpin on impact as the ball enters the pocket. This helps your shot to drive through the rack in a far more efficient manner than a straight shot in which the ball is rolled end over end.

As you improve your ability to throw a hook, you will become more aware of concepts like ball revolutions. There is a direct correlation between the number of revs that you can generate and the amount of hitting power your shot produces. The key ingredient is proper leverage, which derives from your timing and your legs.

To understand this rather simple concept, imagine yourself throwing a baseball. For your first throw, stand square to your target with both of your feet planted on the ground. What little speed results would come entirely from your arm. Now stand slightly sideways and stride forward with your opposite foot as you throw the ball. A big difference, right? Because now you have enlisted the assistance of more of your body to help put more zip on your throw.

Rolling a bowling ball is no different. Your legs are far more powerful than your arms. Unfortunately, very few amateurs take advantage of this principle.

To avoid becoming a part of that unhappy majority, take special care to have a good knee bend with your sliding leg. You will generate far more power when your timing is good and the ball is released close to your sliding foot.

Be certain that your fingers and wrist remain locked throughout. If they are in one position, your leg will help generate power. If your wrist flip-flops during the point of release, the only power on your shot will come from that weaker part of your body.

That doesn't mean that your wrist must remain locked during your entire delivery. Amleto Monacelli's wrist position alters during his armswing. While he's proof positive that it can be done, it's a very tough act to repeat shot after shot. Although that rather unorthodox style works for Amleto, he's very traditional at the point of release. As the ball leaves his hand his wrist muscles are rigid so that it's firmly set into its desired position.

Another key is proper ball speed. Remember, we want our shots to enjoy a skid-roll-hook pattern. Excessive speed will send your ball skidding too far down the lane. Your

*LPBT standout Dana Miller-Mackie intently studies her ball to determine whether she has maintained the consistent speed that is so necessary for good shot making.* Courtesy Ladies Pro Bowlers Tour

ball will never grip the wood sufficiently to gain the drive it needs to power through the pins.

A ball rolled too slowly will hook too soon. By the time it has reached the pins it has used up most of its energy. Instead of driving into the pocket it will weakly deflect.

Your ability to find the happy medium is important. This is yet another reason why a natural armswing is best. If you just let the weight of your ball swing your arm, you will find that you obtain the desired ball speed.

## THE BACK-UP BALL

The hook shot is one that rolls from left to right for a left-handed bowler and from right to left when rolled by a right-handed player. It takes advantage of a variety of your muscles to gain maximum hitting power.

Some newcomers curve the ball in the opposite direction. A lefty will see his or her ball move toward the left and righty watches his or her shot swerve toward the right. The back-up ball is often referred to as a reverse hook but that's a misnomer.

If anything, it should be called a reverse curve. This isn't just a matter of semantics. A hook implies a proper roll in which the ball powers through the pins. But a back-up ball achieves a very limited number of revs. No matter how consistently you learn to roll it, the back-up ball will never generate anywhere near the amount of carrying power as does a hook shot.

The hook, when rolled correctly, takes full advantage of your entire frame—legs, arms, and upper body—to generate its superior striking power. The back-up ball is only aided by a partial exploitation of the leverage from your bowling arm. The ball tracks on the opposite side (on the right side of a right-hander's ball; left on a left-hander's ball).

The back-up is the result of an inside-out motion in which your palm rotates away from your body during the release. The thumb is lower with the fingers higher. Instead of a right-handed player's normal position (fingers at 5 o'clock, thumb at around 2 o'clock), the hand is held two hours "later" (fingers at around 7 o'clock, thumb at around 4 o'clock). The left-hander's digits are two hours "earlier."

But time doesn't fly when you roll the back-up ball. That's because scoring is tougher due to the nature of the shot.

Having said that, I have to add that in many ways it is a more natural way to throw a ball. This seems to be especially true for neophyte female players. The generally accepted theory is that many women's arms face outward at rest, while man's arms and hands tend to hang downward with their palms facing the body.

I'm told that means that all women will naturally feature an inside-out swing in which the hand rotates away from the body (clockwise for a right-handed bowler; counterclockwise for a left-handed player).

Because of the way it's thrown, a back-up ball is inherently limited in the amount of revs it can generate. There are two main impediments to power: the ball is projected away from your center of gravity and your loose wrist fails to take advantage of the potential power from your legs.

Furthermore, the back-up ball and an unrestricted armswing are incompatible. To impart a reverse curve demands that your muscles dominate your swing. This is yet another impediment to achieving both consistency of motion and ball speed.

Finally, most players who roll the back-up do not propel the ball with anywhere nearly enough velocity to take advantage of the sidewalls. Instead of carrying the wall shot strike on light hits, they're often left either with a spare cluster such as the bucket or with a deflection-induced split.

That doesn't mean that you can't achieve a certain level of competence using the back-up. I have seen many local league players who reach the 160–180 plateau with the reverse curve.

Unfortunately for them, they discover that they can only go so far without throwing the ball the "right" way. Having bowled for a considerable period of time to reach their current ability level, they find it harder to make the change to a hook. I suppose the adage about teaching the old dog a new trick applies. The sooner a player scraps the back-up and goes to a hook in his or her bowling career, the easier the change will be.

For those of you who now use the back-up I offer two pieces of advice. Your long-term plans should call for you to eventually trade it for a real hook. This is not a simple alteration, and as such will require hefty dosages of time, patience, and practice.

It will also demand a certain commitment on your part. Your scores are likely to decrease initially as you work to control a hook ball. If you can weather that storm, you will have freed yourself from the limitations of the back-up ball. After all, if it was a viable alternative, you can be sure that at least one of the hundreds of pros on the PBA and LPBT Tours would be throwing it on their strike shots. But they're not. You shouldn't either.

You should no more scrap your back-up ball during a bowling season, however, than a ship should change rudders while in the middle of the ocean. The time to take such a step in your game is when it won't hurt your competitive performance. The off-season, usually the summer, is the best time for instituting a major change in your game.

Which means that if you roll a back-up ball, chances are that you will be stuck with it for some time to come. What to do?

First, at least give yourself the benefit of having your shots angling toward the pins. That means that you should stand on the opposite side of the approach. A left-handed bowler will move far to the right while the right-handed player will use the left side of the approach. You will use the opposite pocket, with lefties aiming for the 1-3 combo while righties try to place their shots in the 1-2 zone.

With the second arrow (in from the gutter) as your

target, your ball will have the optimum entry angle into the pocket.

The danger is that any sort of light hit will be punished. You must be far more accurate than your hook ball opponent if you are to achieve anywhere near the same results.

There is one piece of good news. That natural back-up ball you have acquired does have one useful function. Robin Romeo, who won five tournaments, including the U.S. Open en route to being named the LPBT's 1989 Bowler of the Year, uses the back-up shot to cover her 10-pin conversions. By rolling the ball left to right she lessens the likelihood of a gutter ball as her shot angles toward the target pin.

## TIPS ON HOW TO ROLL AN EFFECTIVE HOOK BALL

OK, so you're determined that the time is now to roll your strike shots the *right* way. How to start?

The key—our previous disclaimer notwithstanding—is to lock your wrist into the same position throughout the entire armswing. Keep your palm directly behind the ball so that it faces the target. During your release your hand should turn slightly inward, about a one-quarter rotation (a right-hander turning counterclockwise).

Your hand goes through the ball before extending fully toward your target. Remember, keep those eyes *riveted* on your target until after the ball has crossed past that point. Closely observe your shot to determine how your ball is reacting to the lane and whether it is driving through the pins or being deflected.

I recommend that beginning players lock their wrist with the hand on the same plane as the arm. The exception is for those of you to whom a cupped wrist feels natural. After you feel comfortable rolling a hook shot you can begin to experiment with cupping that wrist. The more you cup your wrist, the greater the amount of hook.

Take care, however, to make sure that the equipment you're using is the proper weight for your strength level. If you attempt to cup a ball that is too heavy for you to handle, you could end up injuring your tendons.

Never "top" the ball. While it's OK to rotate your hand one-quarter of a turn counterclockwise (for a righty) or clockwise (lefty), your thumb shouldn't point downward during your release. Don't be fooled by the ball's movement. There is a big difference between a hook and a ball that spins. The latter has a smaller tracking ring, which translates into far less carrying power.

The ideal track for today's modern urethane-era game is what is referred to either as the semiroller or the three-quarter roller. That's when the ball tracks to the side of the thumb and finger holes (a right-handed player's ball has the track to the left of the holes and vice versa for a left-handed player).

That's a different philosophy from the conventional thinking of the previous generation that relied on the full-roller. That was a roll in which the track of the ball cut between the thumb and the finger holes. It was thrown with the palm facing upward and the thumb rotating away from the body (the right-handed player's thumb rotated clockwise, left-handers counterclockwise).

I struggle to think of any prominent player on either of today's Tours who still uses the full roller. It has become virtually extinct because it just doesn't generate as much carrying power as does the three-quarter variety.

## A CHANGE IN GRIPS CAN HELP

A large part of the hooking action occurs because your thumb exits the ball first with your fingers providing the lift that's needed during your release to achieve the desired result. A way to keep your fingers in the ball even longer vis-à-vis the thumb is to switch to a fingertip-grip ball.

The fingertip grip is drilled in such a manner that your digits enter only up to the first joint. Often augmented by friction-inducing ball grips that are placed in the holes, this helps to greatly increase the amount of revs that you will obtain.

There is one danger. What you gain in power could be sacrificed in accuracy. I strongly recommend that you do not make this change until you are at least a 150-average player who can control a normal hook ball. Furthermore, certain grips can cause tendon problems. Injuries to both pros and once-a-week amateurs are common and needless. As with all other equipment matters, you are well advised to seek the counsel of a knowledgeable pro shop proprietor.

## THE FINAL WORD ON HOOKERS

Pros like Bob Handley who cover a great number of boards on their strike shots are often jokingly referred to in the

*For the majority of bowlers, accuracy, not power, is the key factor in being successful.* Dan Chidester

locker room as "big hookers." Maybe that's because they're well paid for their services and their style seems very appealing.

For the typical bowler who is lucky to roll more than once a week, a more helpful role model is a player whose shots are more direct. For a Bob Handley to have been so successful requires a tremendous amount of practice so that he is able to consistently repeat his movements.

The ability to be accurate will pay far greater dividends than the carrying power you gain from becoming a big hooker. The key is no different from what it takes to be a good bowler in general: fundamental soundness coupled with lots of practice.

# 8
# *Practicing with a Purpose*

The route to winning the Firestone Tournament of Champions is no different from the way to get to Carnegie Hall: practice, practice, practice. Whether you're someone who just wishes to add a few pins to a 140 average or a pro honing your skills for a major tournament, you won't realize your goals without paying your dues.

For some reason, the majority of bowlers haven't developed the same good practice habits as their counterparts in other games. It's hard to find anyone who is even half-serious about tennis who hasn't taken lessons from a pro and spent hours working on his or her ground strokes. Have you ever met a golfer who has never visited the practice tee?

A lot of folks mistakenly assume that bowling doesn't require the same level of commitment. As for the minority who do allocate regular practice time into their weekly schedules, most simply roll a few lines rather than concentrate on upgrading a specific aspect of their arsenal.

Perhaps it's because bowling does appear to be relatively simple. However, there's a big difference between something that is simple and something that is easy. If practice wasn't both fruitful and necessary you can bet that I'd spend a lot more of my afternoons fishing for bass and a lot less rolling shot after shot at Crossroads Bowl.

The key ingredients to a successful training session are your determination to improve, your recognition of which flaws in your delivery must be remedied, and your ability to design practice activities that are targeted toward achieving one specific goal.

## IDENTIFYING AND OVERCOMING A PROBLEM AREA IN YOUR GAME

You are suffering through a prolonged slump. Your strike shots are still carrying with a fair degree of efficiency but you are missing the pocket a lot more than usual. You can't seem to throw two balls the same way back-to-back. More-

*Among David's practice techniques is shadow bowling, in which the pins are absent. Here Ozio is working on converting the 10 pin.* Dan Chidester

over, your usually accurate spare shooting hasn't been up
to par.

During your next night of league play you ask a teammate to keep an eye on your shots to see if you are hitting
your target consistently. After the first game you are told
that only three of your strike shot attempts went over the
desired arrow.

You have reached the first step of the diagnostic process. Inaccuracy is the disease, but what is its root cause? It
could be that your timing is off, you are dropping your
bowling shoulder, your armswing isn't straight, or a combination of these. Why not enlist the aid of your mates? Ask
one to watch your shots to report on whether the relationship between your release and your slide is consistent. Ask
another to eye that shoulder while a third stands directly
behind you to analyze your swing.

After two games you are told that your timing isn't bad,

*Having a knowledgeable
pro or a friend observe
your game can help to
detect a flaw.* Dan Chidester

you are fairly solid at the line, but your arm is inconsistent. On one shot it bounces out to the side, another time it's tucked inward.

You are closing in on the killer, but even Dick Tracy hasn't solved your case just yet. You think of all the factors that could cause your swing to go east-west instead of straight. It could be that you are holding the ball in front of the middle of your body during your address, or that you aren't consistent in where you are holding it. Your pushaway could be to the inside or to the outside instead of in a direct line off your shoulder. Perhaps you have unknowingly gotten in the bad habit of muscling your shots rather than allowing your arm to swing freely.

Only when the above questions are addressed can you begin to design a practice to alleviate your ailment. Your observers report that your pushaway is the culprit. It's the major reason that your armswing is in more places than the PBA Tour. You are now halfway on the road toward solving your slump.

To cure your faulty and inconsistent pushaway you will concentrate solely on that part of your delivery during your next practice. First, you get a friend to join you. It's his or her job to stand a few feet behind you and report after each shot whether you have pushed the ball toward your target. You, in turn, concentrate on executing that movement followed by a free armswing. After each shot you compare how you felt you executed your shot with what your friend observed.

It's important that—as in competitive bowling—you watch your ball from when it's released until after it impacts with the pins. This will help your analytical process as you will notice whether you've hit your target, if the ball begins to hook at approximately the same spot on the lane (a different break point tells you that your release or speed or both isn't consistent), and whether your shots are driving through the pins or are being deflected.

Central to it all is regaining that feel of a correct pushaway with the ball projected toward your target. By game's end you have helped establish muscle memory. The habit of executing a correct pushaway and armswing has been reestablished.

This is just one example of how an intelligent approach to problem solving can prove helpful. You have used a logical sequence of steps to identify a shortcoming before working to remedy it. During that process you have utilized your analytical ability, enlisted the observational skills of your teammates, and worked out a specific game plan to concentrate on during your practice session.

*Like many top pros, Dave gives lessons when he's not competing on the PBA Tour.* Dan Chidester

## AN ALTERNATIVE PRACTICE STRATEGY

Let's say you don't have a friend who can accompany you to your practice. What do you do?

There are two possiblilities. One is to seek out the help of a respected local professional. A phone call to the Akron, Ohio, headquarters of the PBA or the Rockford,

Illinois, offices of the LPBT will give you names of pros based in your area. Many of them have their own pro shops and are outstanding teachers.

Another option is to inquire at your home lanes whether they have any specific practice tools designed to help solve your problem. In this case, a special bowling mirror might be just what the doctor ordered. These mirrors are placed above the arrows to allow you to see yourself executing your delivery.

By watching the mirror you will discover if your push-away and your armswing are straight. You don't care what happens to the ball after it leaves your hand as long as you have successfully performed the specific part of your delivery that you have targeted for your practice.

## "SPARE" NO EFFORT

Not every practice has to include devices like mirrors or the help of a coach. Your session could be as simple as rolling shot after shot at a spare that has given you particular difficulty. Inquire at the desk whether it's possible to pay for the lane by the hour while "shadow bowling." To roll without pins can prove helpful. Even if a full deck is facing you, it's still possible to work on your spare shooting.

Let's say the 10 pin has become your nemesis. The more times you've missed it, the less confident you've become. When you are seemingly tapped by a ringing 10 you feel you've lost twice. Not only have you been deprived of a deserved strike, you assume that you are now almost certain to suffer an open frame.

That sort of negative thinking isn't uncommon. It's time to turn the weakest part of your game into a strength. As we said in an earlier chapter, the 10 pin is no more difficult than any other shot. Just roll your ball smoothly over that third arrow and you should make it virtually every time.

Instead of going to a bowling center and rolling three games in which you may be faced with half a dozen 10-pin situations, toss your spare ball first. In every frame you attempt to cover the 10 pin on your first ball. You then roll your strike ball on your second shot. Not only will you get more deliveries for your practice buck, you will also get into a helpful rhythm.

Keep track not of your score, but of how many 10 pins you successfully convert. Should you miss, place a G (for a gutter ball) or an IM (inside miss) in that score box. Circle the G or the IM on each shot in which you missed the 10 pin.

Also note if your unsuccessful attempts were due to missing your target or poor execution or both. If you hit your target and were lined up correctly on the approach your miss could be due to squeezing or dropping the ball on your release or to dropping your shoulder.

Recording each shot allows you to discover the pattern to your unsuccessful attempts. That in turn will help you to design a more fruitful practice regimen.

At the end of the day, write down the number of 10-pin attempts/covers as well as how many were missed to the inside or in the channel. Set realistic goals for yourself. If you now make 50 percent of your 10-pin tries, work to upgrade it to 65 percent. If it's 65 percent, aim for 80 percent. And so on. After a few sessions I'm confident that you will enjoy a significant improvement.

Obviously, the same series of steps can be used to work on any single-pin spare leave as well as the various spare clusters or split possibilities. One of the more interesting innovations in bowling was introduced by the Brunswick Corporation in the late 1980s. Known as Bowler-Vision, it's a computerized system that allows you among other things to program a lane to set up whatever pin or combination of pins you wish to practice.

Although as of this writing the centers equipped with this state-of-the-art system are few, I suspect it's a concept that will prove popular. If there's a center near you with Bowler-Vision you may wish to give it a try for your practice sessions.

One of my favorite spare games is called Low Score. I

attempt to cover a 10 pin with one shot and a 7 pin with the following ball. If possible, I pick them cleanly (without touching any other pins in the rack). I count each pin that is toppled.

A first shot gutter ball counts as a strike while one on my second shot is scored as a spare. Thus, a perfect game is a 20.

The beauty of this game is that it's both a useful practice tool and a lot of fun. It allows you to compete against either yourself or an opponent while working to improve a specific aspect of your game.

## SEEING IS BELIEVING

One of the best ways to determine what has gone wrong with your game is to keep a video record. When you find that you are bowling especially well, have a friend tape you in action. That will give you a measure of comparison after you have yourself taped during a period when you have been struggling.

Taking advantage of a VCR will also allow you to visually notice the difference in your form from that of a top pro who serves as your role model (or should I say *roll* model!). Remember, just because a pro is successful doesn't necessarily mean he or she has a style you should copy. Repetition is the one vital ingredient in our sport and anyone who is naturally gifted and dedicated can learn to repeat movements that might not be by the book.

Since you don't have the luxury of matching these players either for God-given ability potential or for the amount of time that you can spend on the lanes, you should opt to pick a player whose game is based on fundamental soundness. I would suggest comparing your form with the deliveries of Brian Voss, Mike Aulby, Dave Ferraro, Dana Miller-Mackie, Parker Bohn III, Lisa Wagner, Steve Wunderlich, Dave Husted, Tom Crites, Tish Johnson, or Marshall Holman. All of these gifted bowlers are fundamentally sound. The simplicity and correctness of their movements are ideal for emulation.

## PRESSURE IS A PERCEPTION YOU CAN PRACTICE

One thing that a pro and a beginner have in common is knowing all too well that feeling in the pits of our stomachs when it comes time to roll a critical shot. I don't care if it's me needing a strike to win the Firestone Tournament of Champions or you having to cover the 5 pin in the 10th frame of a close league game, the perception of pressure is the same.

If there is a difference between you and me it's that a pro bowler learns from previous situations how to deal with tension. We have to be able to handle pressure; it's our livelihood.

One way is to simulate, as best you can, a game-on-the-line environment in your practice sessions. If you have a vivid imagination, you can picture yourself needing this one key shot to win (or avoid losing) a match. Based on how you fare in the 10th frame of your final game, you can offer yourself a reward (a banana split) or a punishment (a three-mile run, or, if you're really serious about handling pressure, having to listen for an hour to your tape of Roseanne Barr singing the National Anthem!).

A better avenue is to compete. Find a friend to bowl against. The stakes can be cash or something as trivial as a soda coupled with bragging rights. The key is to put yourself into that situation in which you must perform with the outcome at stake.

While I'm between Tour sessions I often roll dollar-a-game matches against my brother, Mark, and Wayne Webb. We compete for up to four hours at a time.

Obviously, winning or losing a buck isn't going to have the same effect as the outcome of a match on television in which tens of thousands of dollars are at stake. Nevertheless, the feeling that I get entering the last frame of a close game isn't as dissimilar as you might guess.

In either situation, my ego is on the line. And, yes, even for one dollar I feel a certain anxiety with which I must deal. The more I'm put in that situation, the better I will handle having to perform in the 10th frame during a match game on the PBA Tour.

I make a point to keep mental notes of not only what occurred on key shots, but why something happened. We all have certain "choke" tendencies. Some of us squeeze the ball or rush the foul line. Others tend to drop their shot during the downswing or pull it inside of their target line. A few bowlers rear up at the foul line.

Whatever your bugaboo, it's caused by a lack of confidence. The first step when you face pressure is to remind yourself of all the times that you made that shot before. If you need a strike to win, picture a time when you buried your ball in the pocket and sent those pins flying. Should a 4 pin stand between you and a victory, remind yourself that you have covered more 4 pins in your life than you can count. Then, as that famous sneaker ad says, just do it.

Because simple nervousness is your number-one enemy it is important to try, as best you can, to avoid thinking of what is at stake. Do not tell yourself something like, "Oh heavens, I need this to win the league" or "I must make this or we'll lose." Instead, concentrate on what you need to do to make a good shot ("OK, I'm going to stay down and hit my target.").

One thing that's been very helpful to me is my attitude. I have developed a reputation as one of the better pressure performers on the PBA Tour. I'm convinced that's due to my approach to key 10th-frame shots. I look forward to being placed in that situation. The reason I compete is that I enjoy competing. I like being put to the test. If you relish the chance to attempt a vital shot you are far less likely to blow it.

Do I come through every time? Of course not. But win or lose I do enjoy having the opportunity to make that critical shot. Should I fail, I simply attempt to analyze what I physically did wrong so that I don't repeat the same mistake in a future pressure situation.

## THE DOTS GAME

As you improve, you will enjoy a practice game that I learned as I was growing up. Known as the dots game, it has you attempt to roll strikes from a number of different angles. It's great for teaching you how to alter your speed and hand positions to change the amount that your shot will hook. You will discover how much more difficult accuracy is to obtain when playing deep inside.

To start, roll your favorite strike shot. Mine is one in which I stand on the 25th board and aim for the second arrow. After you have rolled a specific predetermined number of shots, move five boards in the direction of your sliding foot. (We right-handed players move to our left.)

Once again, after rolling the predetermined number of shots, you move another five boards. And so on until you can move no farther. At that point, go in the opposite direction so that you are playing the gutter (right-handers stand to the right and aim up that first board).

You can also reverse the pattern (moving away from the side of your sliding foot). Or you can stay on a dot until you have either hit the pocket or struck $X$ times (or $X$ consecutive times).

The beauty of the dots game is that it teaches you to become a more versatile player. As you move deeper inside (toward your sliding foot) you have to lessen your speed while probably also cupping your wrist for more hooking power. When you move outside (toward your bowling hand) you will have to decrease your hook by flattening your wrist (or even bending it backward), probably coupled with an increase in ball speed.

As you move your feet you also have to change your aiming point on the lane. Through trial and error you will discover what works best for you. A generally accepted rule is to move your target one board in the same direction for every two boards that you moved with your feet.

For each different board you stand on you should make a note of where you have to aim, the amount of speed required, the degree of angle at which your wrist is cupped (or bent backward), and what hand position change, if any, is required. By memorizing adjustments you will learn how to compensate for the various lane-conditioner patterns you will face during competition.

To gain even more, try this exercise in a wide variety of bowling centers so that you are forced to overcome varying shots when playing the gutter on a very dry lane or when deep inside on a lane that is heavily oiled.

The dots game will also help you reinforce the key fundamental aspects to your delivery such as a good push-away, proper armswing, and the directing of all your movements toward your target.

This is not an exercise for the neophyte player. To benefit you should already have learned how to roll a hook shot and have the ability to be reasonably accurate on a consistent basis. It's my hope that you will sufficiently improve so that this game will prove useful. Put this practice tool in your memory bank until such time as you are ready to take advantage of its implementation.

## A FEW FINAL WORDS ON THE ART OF PRACTICE

The most significant tool you can bring to your practice is a positive attitude. Arrive at the center determined to become a better bowler by the time you leave. Concentrate just as fully on a meaningless shot in an empty bowling center at 9 A.M. as you would when a game is on the line in a packed center during your league play at 9 P.M.

A good training session begins with a proper preparation period and warm-up.

As with your competitive bowling, check your equipment before rolling your first shot. Does your ball (or balls) fit properly or must you either insert or remove tape from the thumbhole? Are there any foreign substances on the bottom of your shoes?

If you have an injury, you may wish to use tape for added support. Seemingly little steps like these have saved pro careers.

*Dave makes use of the ball-return apparatus to help stretch his legs (above and opposite). As with his entire routine, the stretch is held for several seconds (most experts concur that bouncing up and down can cause an injury).* Dan Chidester

Next, stretch the important muscle groups that you will be using. Your legs, arms, and back should be loose before you step onto the approach.

If you aren't sure of how to design a personal stretching routine I recommend that you consult with a sports therapist. I went to one a few years ago when I was suffering from lower back problems. He gave me a series of seesaw rolls and leg raises that has proven invaluable. I

might not still be competing today on the pro Tour had it not been for the series of exercises that he showed to me.

When it comes time to roll your first few shots, do so with caution. I am always careful to be very soft with my initial deliveries until my body has again grown accustomed to the feel of bowling. Only at such a time do I roll all out.

Once it's time to practice, do so with a purpose. As stated at this chapter's start, you should arrive at the lanes having already decided what aspect of your game you will be concentrating your efforts on. Don't try to correct four things at once. If you attempt to correct everything the chances are that you will accomplish nothing. Instead, focus on that one key ingredient in your game that you need to improve.

Really work when you are on the lanes, but do not overpractice. When your concentration begins to fade, take a break. You can get into more bad habits than you will alleviate if you become sloppy.

Finally, try to end your practice on a successful note. It's a great feeling to walk out of the center after throwing

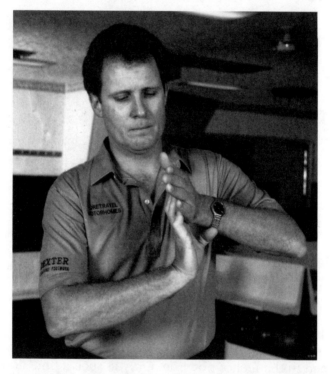

*Stretching the oft-neglected wrist of one's bowling hand is a vital step to help prevent an injury. Dave first pushes the tips of the fingers of his bowling (right) hand forward against his other hand for four seconds. He then relaxes for six seconds before putting pressure with his bowling hand against his left hand for another four seconds. Finally, he applies pressure with the other hand against his bowling hand for six seconds.*

Dan Chidester

**Touching the floor for a 5- to 10-second interval prepares the leg muscles.**

the perfect strike (or even better, a few in a row). The positive attitude and confidence that you will gain from leaving on a high note should carry over to your next competitive session.

# 9
# *The Flawed Brigade*

You know 'em, I know 'em, everyone who bowls knows them. They're the bowlers who aren't bad but who ought to be a whole lot better except that one or two significant shortcomings are preventing them from realizing their potential. In all likelihood, obtaining a 20-pin improvement in their average would not be nearly as difficult as they think.

The good news is that if the bowling shoe fits you don't have to wear it. Most typical bowlers in the 120–150 average range share the following traits:

1. They enjoy bowling but roll only once or twice a week with little time or inclination to practice extensively.
2. They have never seen tapes of themselves in action nor have they taken any lessons from a pro. As a result, any major flaws in their delivery have probably gone undetected.
3. They are often frustrated by inconsistency ("How could I be so good one game and so bad the next?").

Being consistent is an elusive goal even for the finest of players in any athletic activity. While none of us will ever realize our potential in every game we roll, you should be able to achieve a certain minimum standard that you reach or exceed virtually every night. The key to this, as well as to your overall improvement, is to eliminate those idiosyncrasies in your style that make it more difficult for you to repeat the same series of motions shot after shot, game after game.

Perhaps you will see yourself in some of the hypothetical "heroes" that I'm about to describe. If the shoe fits, it's time for you to step up to a better style of bowling.

## AWFUL ARMSWING ALICE

Let's hope there is some comfort to be found in the old adage that misery loves company. To say that you're not alone is a classic understatement.

Take, for example, my friend Awful Armswing Alice (or, as she's known to most, Ms. Swing). By the time it

*Scott Devers has done well on the PBA Tour despite a highly unorthodox game that features a circuitous armswing. Unless you can practice 100–200 games a week like Scott does, you will probably fare better with a more traditional style that's by the book.* Russ Vitale

**Wrapping the armswing behind their back is a common flaw among lower-average players.** Dan Chidester

drops onto the lane, Alice's bowling ball must feel like a rat in a maze searching for a nonexistent piece of cheese.

Alice muscles all of her shots and her arm wraps behind her back. That forces her hand to take a circuitous route forward as she prepares to release her shot.

The height of her backswing varies, so the speed of Alice's shots is wildly inconsistent. Whenever her timing is less than perfect on a shot the ball flies off to the side. When Alice is subjected to pressure things break down entirely.

Alice's predicament reminds me of Sam Snead's famous line that most people would starve to death if they gripped a knife and fork the way they do a golf club. The state of most bowlers' armswings is no better.

Remember that the key to a good armswing is two-fold. First, execute a proper pushaway in which the ball is handed forward toward your target and slightly upward on a plane just outside of your hip. Second, allow gravity to naturally make your arm act as a pendulum with your shoulder as the fulcrum.

In the chapter on how to practice more effectively, I related some ways to improve this vital aspect of your delivery. Having observed more amateur players than I could possibly count, I feel safe in stating that poor arm-swings are an extremely prevalent hindrance to the major-ity of middle- and lower-average players.

## *FAST FEET FREDDIE*

If bowling was a track meet this guy would win hands down. He gets to the line so fast that it's amazing sparks

*Dave poses as Fast Feet Freddie. Notice how his dash to the line has resulted in his turning sideways to the foul line as he releases his shot.* Dan Chidester

don't fly from his shoes. Had only a football scout been on hand Freddie would surely be offered a no-cut contract as a cornerback or a split end.

Because his body moves so rapidly toward the foul line, it's virtually impossible for him to execute a smooth delivery. He flings his shots at the pins instead of rolling them. Like Alice, he finds consistency an elusive goal.

Freddie's solution is obvious: slow down! He can practice his footwork without a ball.

If you are a Freddie, I suggest that you concentrate on starting your delivery with a slow and short first step. The succeeding strides should increase moderately in both length and tempo so that you are still moving at a controlled pace as you reach the foul line. You Freddies can even use a mirror at home to make certain that you're meeting the proper timing checkpoints throughout your delivery.

With time, your slower style will put you in scoring's fast lane. You will find that acquiring a tempo to your motions allows you to be far smoother. That in turn will translate into shots that are both more powerful and more accurate.

## WEAK WRIST WILMA

You don't need a body builder's forearms to be a good bowler. But if your musculature is seriously deficient, you had better take some steps to compensate.

Wilma's problem is that the wrist of her bowling hand flip-flops under the weight of a ball that is too heavy for her body type. Her wrist motion hinders her efforts to be accurate. It also produces an inadequate roll, which causes her shots to weakly deflect after impacting against the pins.

The first step for you Wilmas is to get a ball that fits your hand correctly and is the right weight for you. Next, you need to be more aware of locking your wrist into one position throughout your entire armswing and follow-through.

If you find that you just can't achieve that goal, consider purchasing a wrist aid device or using tape for added support. While I'm not the biggest of fans of most wrist paraphernalia on the market, there are some players who are aided by using a wrist support device.

## DEAD DROP DIANE

A dead drop is not to be confused with the rather unhealthier malady of dropping dead. Nevertheless, it's almost as injurious to your game's health.

One thing is for sure—unless you have lots of cotton stuffed into your ears you don't want to be in the basement when Diane is bowling. Her ball is dropped onto the lane with a bang that probably registers on the Richter scale.

Diane is a nice person but she's stiff. That sliding leg of hers is locked as tight as a bank vault on Saturday night.

You Dianes need to slide smoothly with a bend in your knee. Your hand should stay behind the ball instead of on top of it. Those things should be coupled with a concerted effort to roll the ball over the foul line. Doing so will not only help you to become more accurate, it will give your ball a lot better roll to be better able to power through the pins.

## BENT ELBOW BARNEY

If you must bend your elbow at the lanes, do it between frames while enjoying a soft drink. A textbook armswing is level with your elbow being in the flat position.

A bent elbow means that you must use muscle power for your swing. As we have noted (several times for emphasis!), this is not desirable. Let that arm swing freely. To do so, the elbow must be straight.

If your elbow is bent, one of two other things must occur to compensate and both of them are bad. Your hand is likely to release the ball too far from the ground. You will lose leverage at the point of release, your ball will have a poorer roll after it has crashed into the lane, and you won't be able to obtain any appreciable degree of ball speed.

To compensate, in an effort not to drop his shot, Bar-

**Keep that elbow straight if you want to execute a proper armswing.** Dan Chidester

ney might bend too much from his waist to get that hand closer to the floor. That will make it very difficult to eye his target throughout his delivery. He will probably release the ball during his downswing. The result is also a much weaker roll than had the ball been released properly. Barney will suffer by getting less carrying power than had he not bent his arm.

Does that mean that you absolutely can't bowl successfully with a bent elbow? Hardly. As with all aspects of tenpins, there have been unorthodox players who have enjoyed astounding success. Foremost among the "Barney brigade" is none other than all-time great Don Carter.

As exceptional a performer as Carter was in his day, I suspect that he would have to modify this aspect of his delivery if he competed in the contemporary era. In his day, slow ball speed was almost a prerequisite. Today's conditions call for being able to roll shots with considerably more pace. No matter how strong you might be, there is only so much ball speed you can obtain with a bend in your arm.

Keeping that elbow straight isn't difficult. Let the ball swing your arm. You can practice by allowing that ball to swing freely as you stand still. Grow accustomed to the feeling and it will no longer seem awkward to let the ball—and not your muscles and definitely not your elbow—bear the brunt of the strain.

## CRANKING CARL

When this guy is hot the pins stand about as much chance of surviving as a third-rate club fighter would with Mike Tyson. As he arrives at the foul line Carl puts every ounce of energy into hitting his release. Both his strike and spare balls hook from here to Saskatchewan. They have enough revs to win the Indianapolis 500.

There is just this one little problem. Poor Carl can't hit

*Cranking Carl hurls a shot that is literally over the arrows. Control and accuracy, not excessive speed, get results.* Dan Chidester

the broad side of a barn three times out of every four deliveries. A right-handed player, he's terrified of the 10 pin. Given a choice, Carl would prefer to work for George Steinbrenner than have to convert that spare with a game on the line. So wide is his hook that he can hit a few boards in either direction and still strike, but he must seemingly split hairs to cover that pesky corner pin. And his strike shot's sharp entry angle into the pins makes that ringing 10-pin leave more likely.

Carl, my friend, it's time to change your ways.

Any player who can even approach Carl's level of power must possess a fair amount of natural athletic ability. You should not have a lower average than people who are nowhere as athletically gifted as you are.

The first step is no more complex than recognizing a key fact of bowling life: style points (à la gymnastics) are not awarded in tenpins. That blow-'em-away strike is impressive, perhaps even intimidating to some opponents. It is a great weapon when utilized by a Pete Weber because he combines it with consistent accuracy.

Power is not an asset if it is obtained at the expense of control. Part of the maturation process from being a prospect on the PBA Tour to becoming an accomplished professional is learning how to hit the pocket more often.

That's an even greater trait on those occasions when difficult lane conditions significantly decrease one's margin for error. The rule is that the lower the scoring is, the more direct a strike line you should use. When it comes to competing on a grind-'em-out condition, players like our friend Carl are totally lost.

Instead of trying to destroy the pins, be content merely to entice them to fall down. Try to be smooth throughout your delivery. The less herky-jerky your movements, the better. Do not excessively cup that wrist. Keep your hand locked in one position behind the ball throughout your swing, or at most execute just the slightest rotation.

Yes, your carry percentage on pocket hits will decrease slightly. But that will be more than offset by hitting the pocket far more often.

## CUT 'EM OFF CATHY AND CURSE 'EM OUT KEN

Nice girl, this Cathy, but with some rather annoying habits that make her a pain to bowl with.

Knocking over pins is half the battle. Observing bowling etiquette is also important if all involved are to experience an enjoyable night at the lanes.

Cathy is one of those types who is never around when you need her, such as when it's her turn to bowl. She could be at the snack bar ordering up some fries, on the phone chatting with a friend, or 20 lanes away shooting the breeze. It seems that in every other frame she makes everyone else wait.

One of the most difficult aspects of league play is trying to maintain some sort of rhythm when you must wait four or five minutes between turns. That's a tough enough challenge without the added delay caused by inconsiderate folks. By the time the player in front of you completes his or her frame, you should be standing and ready to step onto the approach.

Cathy's other annoying habit is her failure to yield the right of way to others. Before you take that ball out of the rack you should check to make certain that the lane to either side of you is clear. If two players are ready simultaneously, the bowler on the right goes first. Eye contact and a simple nod of the head are the communication tools of choice. Once it is established that it's your turn to roll, please waste no time in executing your delivery.

You can say this for Cathy, she may not be much on manners but her shortcomings are inadvertent and probably caused by ignorance. A word to the wise offered in a constructive manner is usually sufficient to obtain the desired results.

Ken, however, is a different story. Even though he is not a very good bowler, nor is he exactly bursting with dedication and great practice habits, he expects to roll a strike every time. Let Ken think that he's been tapped and some ball return unit will pay the price by absorbing a swift kick. His vocabulary is varied, although not very

*Proper etiquette calls for waiting until the player on the adjacent lane has completed his or her shot before you step onto the approach.* Dan Chidester

much of it can be found on these pages. Worst of all, he seems to save his most dramatic tantrums for just when others are in the middle of their deliveries on an adjacent lane.

Ken, in short, is a jerk. He thinks his anger makes him appear to be a great competitor. Nothing could be further from the truth.

His actions are not only rude and inconsiderate, they're illegal. Check the rule book and you will see that there are sanctions for players who do things like fouling intentionally after missing a spare (they get a zero for the entire frame!).

If these types don't respond to reasonable requests to behave, they should be reported to your league president. Idiots like that have no place in bowling and deserve to be tossed out of your league. It's up to you to determine what sort of atmosphere prevails in the place you spend your leisure time. I can't imagine that bowling will be as pleasurable as it should be if you tolerate Ken's behavior. As for me, I find nothing enjoyable about being subjected to distracting and rude antics.

## IMMOBILE IKE

Ike's a predictable chap. On his strike shots you will always find him standing in the same place and aiming at the same target. He must subscribe to the Emancipation Proclamation of Tenpins ("All lanes are created equal").

Unfortunately for Ike, unlike him, oil does move. When the lane conditioner evaporates, so do Ike's scores. His strategy makes as little sense as a golfer using a driver to tee off on every hole, including on short par 3s.

One of the biggest shortcomings of middle-average amateurs is this inability to play the lane. Try different lines during your warm-up period to discover which yields the greatest margin for error. And by all means work hard on the dots game during practice sessions so that you are versatile enough to execute a wide variety of strike shot lines.

## A FINAL WORD

I hope that if you have seen yourself in some of the above descriptions you can work to improve. If you are a Curse 'Em Out Ken, please change your ways. You'll find that as your ranting decreases, so will your blood pressure. Chances are your scores will increase.

The point of this chapter wasn't to be cute with nicknames. Nor was it to test how alert you Flintstones fans are. You Bedrock folks may be wondering why I mentioned Fred, Wilma, and Barney only to forget about Betty (perhaps we can deal with Ms. Rubble in a future text).

The idea was to personify qualities in players that are common hindrances to better scoring. If you bowl with any degree of regularity you will develop a certain level of muscle memory. The good news is that will make it less difficult to repeat the same series of motions. That ability to achieve repetition is an important ingredient toward being successful.

The bad news is that it also means you are likely to repeat the same mistakes. The first substantive step toward improving is to identify an area of your delivery that isn't up to par. I recommend either studying yourself on tape or having a qualified instructor observe you in action.

Having noted your major shortcomings, work hard to overcome your flaws. Fast feet and muscled armswings are extremely common. Both are not that difficult to eliminate. All that is required is to identify the problem and design purposeful practice sessions. Mix that together with un-bridled determination not to be discouraged if your scores decrease in the short term.

Knowing how to bowl is half the battle. Realizing what pitfalls you must avoid and overcoming them is the other half. Good luck.

# 10
# Common
# Misconceptions

Remember when you were in grade school and some advanced pal filled you in on his or her version of the facts of life? Chances are that you were fed a lot more misinformation than information. So it is with people who learn to play this game by observing and listening to others who aren't particularly good bowlers.

If knowledge is the key then ignorance is the lock. Incorrect concepts abound in bowling, probably because so few players ever take the time to get lessons from qualified instructors. This chapter is dedicated to shooting down myths, misconceptions, and half-truths.

**To become a good bowler you must be able to hook the ball from here to China.** Wrong! Wrong! Wrong!

Knock down a lot of pins and you're good. Style points count in figure skating, not in figuring scoring.

Most people who start bowling fall in love with the big hook. That's what you see many players doing on TV. There is a certain sex appeal attached to the ball that rockets into the pins and sends them scattering in all directions. It's got the same charisma as a slam dunk in basketball or a tape measure home run.

But you will never see a great hitter who swings for the fences on every pitch. There are situations that call for trying to hit to the opposite field or for laying down a bunt.

The truly exceptional pro bowler can throw a big hook. But he or she keeps it under control. And he or she is equally efficient when rolling the ball straight to cover certain spares.

*Getting proper instruction from a qualified pro early on helps you to avoid harboring common (and harmful) misconceptions.* Dan Chidester

Too much hook can be counterproductive. The more boards your ball crosses, the less accurate you are likely to become. Spraying is good for killing insects. It's not nearly as useful for knocking over pins. While a straight ball isn't the answer, neither is an excessive hook an asset.

There are some things you can be absolutely sure will occur every year on the PBA Tour: bowlers will complain about lane conditions, fans will ask you for an autograph at the darnedest times and places (I have been approached while in the men's room), and some rookie with a big hook ball will be in for the shock of his young life.

These guys come on Tour with expectations the size of the Empire State Building but without enough talent to fill a studio apartment. They can throw strikes on easy oil patterns back home even when they miss their target by several inches. That 235 average on easy lane conditions leads them to believe that they are the second coming of Mark Roth.

When I made my less-than-overwhelming Tour debut in 1978 I had averaged 240 during the first 60 games of my league season. I then went out and averaged all of 206 in PBA events. For me, as for countless others, competing with the big boys on their own turf came as a rude awakening.

Strikes aren't as easy to come by on our lane conditions. The top players cover their spares virtually every time. Many of the superstar-back-home types have never worked on their spare games. After all, why practice something you are almost never faced with because your name is always followed by a series of *X*s?

It takes about two or three tournaments for reality to sink in. In Tour parlance, the player is sent home. Many are never heard from again. The better ones work on their weaknesses and learn how to throw their shots with less hook without sacrificing carrying power. When they have successfully married power with accuracy, they have become legitimate contenders for PBA honors.

That's not to say that a big hook is inherently bad. I believe in the beer theory of bowling: treat the hook ball like any other intoxicating item—never use more than you can control and only use it on appropriate occasions.

The other end of the spectrum is no bargain, either. If you don't throw enough hook, you won't carry as well. There is a happy medium.

The problem with the straight-as-an-arrow shot is that it is rolled end over end or with hardly any rotation. When ball meets headpin the former will tend to deflect instead of driving through the rack. Unless you have hit the pocket completely flush, you won't carry.

Good bowling technique is all about increasing your margin for error. The straight ball that is a bit light is less likely to result in a strike than a powerful hook ball that barely touches the headpin.

The trade-off between maximum accuracy (straight ball) or power (big hook ball) is to find a happy medium in which you generate the latter without sacrificing the former. One without the other is about as useful as a fancy sports car sans engine or gasoline.

Accuracy's importance is self-evident. Power (which, as previously noted, is *not* to be mistaken as identical to maximum hook or ball speed) is also a vital ingredient to success.

The desired set of events that should occur on a pocket hit (your ball takes out the four central sticks while the headpin and 3 pin set off a chain reaction to knock over the flank pins) will be altered by ball deflection. A properly released shot will generate sufficient revs (ball revolutions) to either eliminate or at the very least minimize deflection.

Remember, the failure to do so causes your ball to hit too much of the 3 pin (2 pin for you lefties), causing it to fly backward instead of sideways. The result is a weak corner pin leave. Your ball might also miss the 5 pin entirely, or it might nick the 5 pin and deflect again to leave the 8 pin. Worse still are combinations of the above that end up with you facing a deflection split (5-7, 8-10).

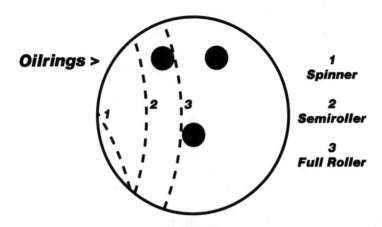

**You can tell how much power your shots have by how much your ball's path curves.** This is a half-truth. Most power players do cover a lot of boards, but not all bowlers who cover a lot of boards are power players. A spinner can cover the same circuitous route to the pocket as a hook ball, but it won't give you sufficient power.

How can you tell if your ball is grabbing the lane or skidding over it? After your ball is returned, take a look at the oil ring. As you can see from the accompanying illustration, the ring can be small (line 1) or large (2). When it comes to bowling, I partially subscribe to the Mr. T theory—(bigger rings are better).

The small ring the size of a softball means that your shot has spun somewhat like a top. If you played with one of those toys as a kid, you know that the slightest breeze could knock it over. Not enough ball surface on the lane has the same effect. To take full advantage of inertia, a bigger ring is required.

The spinner is usually caused by an improper hand position at the point of release. Your hand should be behind the ball, *not* on top of it. Remember, start those fingers behind the ball and rotate them slightly during your release. If they are improperly positioned your ball could spin like a top.

A curve is not the same as a hook. Just because your shot has made a little turn toward the pocket does not mean your hand was in the right place. Make certain that your hand position is right so that power can be obtained from both your fingers and your legs.

There is a point where too big a track area becomes a detriment. The full roller (line 3) was popular in my dad's heyday.

The full roller results when you lift straight upward at your point of release. The common expression is to say that the player comes through the ball. The thumb points downward before the fingers rotate clockwise (for right-handers). You hold the ball in the same manner that you would grasp a suitcase.

The full roller is a shot that you should pack away. Where the semiroller is able to take full advantage of your ball's top weight, the old-fashioned approach does not. It fails to fully exploit the benefit of having an extra weight block at the ball's top for added finishing power. I can't think of a single modern professional of any appreciable stature who doesn't use the semiroller. In fact, every player on the Tour except Tom Baker throws that three-quarter roller because it's far more powerful.

Carrying power is more a function of the type of roll imparted on the ball than the numbers of boards covered. Several PBA stars who roll relatively straight shots are among the leaders in ratio of strikes per pocket hits. I would count myself in that category along with Brian Voss and Tony Westlake.

We all have what is known as heavy roll. That has nothing to do with our breakfast preference and everything to do with hitting the pins hard. You can roll a ball on line like a Walter Ray Williams, Jr., and still generate a strong roll.

The key to obtaining heavy roll is to have your hand cleanly exit from the ball. Your shot must be smoothly projected onto the lane. Having your thumb hang in the hole or dropping the ball during your release are guaranteed ways to ruin the roll.

**The hook ball is always an asset.** Not so. It certainly is disadvantageous in any situation in which accuracy, not power, is at a premium. You don't need power to knock over a single-pin spare. Even my three-year-old daughter can do that every time her ball makes contact with the pin, even though you could just about eat a hot dog in the time it takes for her shots to travel from foul line to the pit. Except with double wood, you don't have to overpower a spare. You just have to hit the target pin.

Nor is a hook great on a real tough condition. Remember that the rule is the lower the scoring, the fewer boards your shots should cover.

There are lane conditions in which the oil pattern allows for virtually no margin for error. On an easy condition, the typical pro may be able to strike even if he or she missed the target by a board or two in either direction. There are even some houses in which power players can be off by a full arrow (five boards) and still hit the pocket.

But on a "grindout" condition, in which the margin for error is slight and scoring is low, a one- or two-board error can be very costly. With accuracy elevated to paramount importance, even the highly talented pros opt to roll far straighter. If you find you are having trouble being accurate, it's a good idea to cut down on the amount of hook on your shot.

Keep in mind that the stars you see on television have rolled tens of thousands of games to get where they are today. The great amount of practice they have endured allows them to better control a big hook. You would be amazed how much more direct even big hook players like Marshall Holman and Amleto Monacelli roll shots as veterans compared to their early years as pros. They and players like them have learned that accuracy, not power, promotes consistency.

The ability to keep the ball in play is the major reason why most pros lose an average of a board per year on their hook.

It's my conviction that all entry-level players and those intermediate bowlers who don't practice a lot are far better

**LPBT star Aleta Sill gets great results from her smooth delivery. She saves the fast balls for baseball pitchers.** Courtesy Ladies Pro Bowlers Tour

advised to concentrate on hitting their target. Until you average at least 180, your primary goal should be to fill as many frames as you can. Remember, you can shoot a 190 without the benefit of a single strike. Power without accuracy is far less desirable than accuracy without power.

If you have very little hook or you roll the ball straight, you can increase your carrying power by using angles to better advantage. Start close to the gutter on the side of your bowling hand and point your shot at the pocket. By drawing an imaginary line from your hand to the pocket you will discover an aiming point on the lane where the line intersects the arrows.

For a dead-straight ball I would recommend the 12th or 13th board as a good starting position for your feet. Since you will probably release your ball about five to seven boards to the right of your foot position, a shot over the second arrow should normally hit the pocket.

**The harder you throw, the more pins will go**. Wrong again! As I noted earlier, speed may not kill but it doesn't always help. Throwing shots harder doesn't mean you will knock down more pins. In fact, the opposite can be true.

The greater your ball speed, the more skid and less roll you will get on your shot. More important, excessive speed can cause the front pins to fly over (instead of into) those in the back row. Rocketmen often scream of being "robbed" by the solid 10 pin when a little less speed might have helped the 6 pin to hit the corner stick instead of flying around its neck.

Excessive speed has become a greater liability when today's pins, which are lighter, are met with today's urethane balls, which are far more powerful than their plastic and rubber predecessors.

One of the keys to being accurate with a hook ball is to maintain consistent ball speed. This is another reason that a hook of moderate proportions is more advantageous. No matter how good a player you may become, it is virtually impossible to throw every shot at exactly the same speed. Balls that are rolled slower than usual will hook more while faster ones will cover fewer boards.

If Player A hooks his regular shot twice as much as Player B, a moderate change in speed will result in Player A being twice as far off target. Player B may go one board high if her shot is a bit slower, thus leaving the 4 pin. But Player A will miss by two boards and that might mean being faced with a difficult split.

If they both roll a shot too hard, Player A might miss the headpin altogether. If his approaching ball angle is great (as most big hook players' tend to be), he could be faced with a washout (1-2-10) or a light-hit split (2-10). Player B will probably nick the headpin and thus have a far less difficult conversion.

If you must err, it's better to roll the ball on the firm side. Speed, within reason, is an asset. We have all seen what happens when a ball rolled by a three-year-old finally reaches the end of its journey after a 15-second stroll down the lane.

Insufficient speed—even if not to that degree—can also cause deflection. Adequate speed allows pins to ricochet off the sidewalls and back into play. Thus, one can carry what is known as the wall shot strike. That occurs on a light hit with a good roll in which the headpin flies into the left sideboard before rebounding to eliminate the 4, 5, and 7 pins.

Fast is better than slow but faster is no bargain. Aside from carrying half-hits, you run the risk of being out of control. There have been times when I have fallen into that trap.

When lanes become drier the ball hooks too much. To counter that while on Tour, my normal adjustment is either to switch to a harder-shell ball (for less hook) or to roll my

*Following Dave's advice might not get you quite this far, but it will help you to become the best player you can be.* Russ Vitale

shots faster. Be careful not to throw the ball too hard or you might find yourself off balance during your delivery.

This is another area where equipment is a factor. If your ball is too light for your level of strength, you are more likely to begin winging your shots. Conversely, a ball that is heavier than you can control will make it even more difficult for you to generate a sufficient minimum level of ball speed.

**Lofting is a good technique for getting your ball through the head area of the lane to avoid early hook**. There are some knowledgeable people who subscribe to the above but this pro isn't among them.

There are better ways to accomplish that objective. To impart loft your hand must stay in the holes of the ball past the leverage point. It diminishes the roll on the ball, so you sacrifice vital effectiveness and hitting power.

A smooth release coupled with a long follow-through is the formula for a delivery with the best chance to prohibit your ball from rolling early.

# 11
# Tips for Juniors and Seniors

Current PBA superstar Pete Weber produced his first perfect game at age 12. American Bowling Congress Hall of Fame member Joe Norris is still rolling them well into his 80s. Ours is a sport that places no restrictions on age.

One of the nicest aspects of tenpins is that it's a game you can play virtually your entire life. And it's one that you can take up at almost any stage of your life. Either way, with a few concessions to the calendar it can be even more fun.

As a kid I practically lived at the lanes. I spent all week anxiously awaiting my Saturday morning youth league. By the time I'd reached my teens, I was involved with several leagues. If there is one common trait that most of us who have been successful on the PBA Tour share, it's a love for the game. We became as good as we are because we grew up *wanting* to spend time practicing instead of *having* to practice.

## TWO TENPIN EXAMPLES THAT AGE IS BUT A STATE OF MIND

That same love of bowling was probably already in Joe Norris's blood when he was born in 1908. Here is a man

*Joe Norris's remarkable career spanned almost the entire 20th century. Here he receives a golden pin from former American Bowling Congress president Paul Mohn (right) after Joe toppled his 100,000th pin in ABC Tournament competition.* Courtesy American Bowling Congress

who still averages close to 200 at an age when most people would be content just to be alive. Very few players even half his age can compete with Joe. Joe placed among the top finishers in the All Events category of the 1927 American Bowling Congress Tournament. In the same year, Charles Lindbergh became the first to fly solo nonstop across the Atlantic Ocean and Babe Ruth hit a then record-breaking 60 home runs.

To put Joe's amazing longevity feats into perspective, he was competing at the highest level before all but a handful of the current PBA Senior Tour players were born. And he's still going strong.

I don't think there are too many octogenarians who can reasonably expect to either remain or become scratch bowlers. But Joe does prove that there is no reason that you older readers can't do well far into your golden years.

Nor is Joe Norris the only role model for older players.

*Remarkable Hall of Fame member Dick Weber won his first PBA title in 1959 and his most recent (as of press time) in 1989, just before his 60th birthday.* Courtesy Professional Bowlers Association

Pete's dad, Richard Anthony Weber, remains one of the most incredible sports personalities I have ever come across. He's told me that one of his goals is to win a tournament in the 1990s (he'll probably have done that before you read this book!). When that occurs he will have captured at least one PBA title in five different decades. Dick Weber has been named to *Bowling* magazine's first unit All-America team 11 times.

Mr. Weber turned 60 in 1989. In addition to still being a formidable competitor on those occasions when he enters a PBA tournament, he is also fighting for the all-time earnings lead on the Senior Tour.

Bowling against him is a tough chore. Not only is he still extremely talented, he's a hero to many of today's pros. We all learned the hard way not to let the bowling fan inside of us take over when we face him or we'll get our butts kicked. His son, Pete, may be one of the top stars today but he knows that even he is in for a battle when he bowls against his old man. Whatever Dick Weber may have lost to the years is offset by the same tremendous desire to compete.

## ADMIT, BUT DON'T ACT, YOUR AGE

As amazing as they are, even Dick and Joe have to make some changes to accommodate being a senior. Foremost of these is that Joe no longer uses a 16-pound ball. As he's aged he has gradually decreased the weight of his equipment. Although that does somewhat hinder his carrying power, Joe's ability to maintain control over his shots has allowed him to retain a great degree of the accuracy that has helped to make him such a great player.

The need to use a lighter ball can be tough on the ego. Nobody wants to admit that age has gotten the better of us. It's human nature to want to act as young as possible and not to be perceived by others as having aged significantly.

Many older males refuse to concede that they no longer have enough strength to handle the maximum allowable ball weight. They continue to use a ball that is harder for them to control. After a game or two they become fatigued, which leads to poorer play.

Ironically, hardly anyone would notice a switch to a lighter ball (you can still get it in the same color) but virtually everyone will recognize the declining scores. If you want to appear to be young, admit (only to yourself!) that you're not quite as youthful as you once were.

Another key is to have established good habits throughout your bowling years. While it might not seem necessary to most younger players to stretch your wrist, arms, and legs prior to bowling, it is a smart step to take. Stretching to help prevent needless injuries becomes more important as we all become older.

Our ability to concentrate for prolonged periods diminishes as we age. Joe has found that bowling with top-quality players helps him to retain his sharpness. By talking about your game between shots you are better able to stay focused.

At the other end of the equation is your ability to still have every bit as much fun bowling as you did when it was a bit easier to knock over pins. As life expectancy has increased dramatically in this century, more and more seniors are leading active lifestyles. Many bowling centers have seniors-only leagues.

The proprietors with whom I have spoken tell me that it isn't always easy to convince people to join, but once they do they have a fantastic time. I'm told that the hardest selling job involves players with solid averages who have always enjoyed the competition that bowling offers.

Remember, there is no law against bowling in both your regular leagues and a seniors circuit. You will probably have an even greater time given that you will be surrounded by newfound friends who share a lot of common interests. Admit it, wouldn't it be nice to spend active time with others who grew up in the same era as you and probably share your taste in theater, movies, and music? These are folks who lived through the same history you did as opposed to people who vaguely recall incidents as something they read in a book in some high school social studies class.

Besides, you might just be surprised to find that you aren't the only one on the second side of 60 who is still able to hold your own on the lanes.

For every Joe Norris and Dick Weber there are thousands of others who didn't start to bowl until their later years. Most of these types are drawn by the social nature of the game. If that's how you got started I say that it's great. But don't limit yourself to just having fun. Find a quality instructor and spend some time practicing so that you can improve. Unlike old dogs, old bowlers *can* learn new tricks.

## TIPS ON TEACHING YOUR CHILD TO BOWL BETTER

I also have some advice for the future seniors like Haleigh Ozio and Colin Herbst, who will each turn 65 in 2053. The main thing for my coauthor's son is to do what his old man and I do: enjoy our bowling.

*If you can walk you are old enough to bowl, and bumpers just add to the fun!* Dan Chidester

So many of my fondest childhood memories are of times spent on the lanes. One of the biggest kicks I get is that parental thrill of watching my two daughters smiling from ear to ear as they bowl. Almost overnight they graduated from plastic pins to the real thing; from pushing the ball on their knees to using one hand.

To you parents, I strongly encourage you to urge your children to bowl. Take them at every opportunity. It's a marvelous way for a family to spend time together. From talking with a lot of my fellow pros who are parents of older children, I've discovered that an added bonus is that there are many very valuable lessons that youngsters learn from bowling.

Early on they can be taught that there are several rules that they must obey when playing a game. The two-year-old who has a very limited attention span learns how to take turns and that she can't run all over the place. Having to share ("It's your sister's turn now, you bowl after

Daddy") isn't easy at a stage when a child wants what she wants when she wants it.

Bowling helps lengthen a child's attention span. After a few frames many kids are off to a video game or a snack bar. At a relatively young age a child can be taught that those needs will be taken care of only *after* this game has ended. Trying to teach patience to a young child is never easy, but it's a less difficult concept to impart at a bowling center.

Make sure you help your child to learn proper etiquette. Along that line, please don't push your child to become bowling's next superstar. Kids don't need to learn how to win or any of those other stupid clichés. If they have fun when they bowl poorly in addition to enjoying their good days they will be well served. Chances are they will become better players because of that.

Part of the growth process of playing sports is learning how to handle disappointment. I find it very discouraging when a school-age player misbehaves after throwing a bad shot. I'm far more impressed with junior bowlers who behave well than I am by those with higher averages but lower sportsmanship.

An interviewer once asked former tennis great Bjorn Borg why he was so much better behaved on the court than some of the others in his game. Bjorn replied that as a kid he threw fits until his father took his racket away for one month. Not being able to engage in his favorite activity for that long taught him a lesson that has lasted a lifetime.

Sanctions in youth sports need not be so severe for initial and minor transgressions. Just the threat of a loss of a turn for misbehaving helps you to impart social values to your child.

## AN AMAZING INNOVATION

In the past, young kids had to learn how to deal with frustration when gutter balls outnumbered shots that hit wood. That no longer has to be the case.

One of the greatest inventions has to be bumper bowling. Inflatable tubes are placed into both gutters so that every shot stays in play. This allows your child to enjoy the thrill of knocking over pins more often.

When bumpers were first introduced some people were skeptical whether bumper bowling wouldn't spoil youngsters. How would a kid who is accustomed to hitting wood on his or her shots feel about rolling gutter balls after reaching an age when the bumpers were removed? Would that kid become disillusioned and discouraged?

The answers, I'm happy to say, show that kids are more mature than we adults usually give them credit for being. The reaction of the children I've seen is to be proud of being such an older and experienced bowler that they no longer need the bumpers. Very few seem upset when their scores go down. They realize they are now bowling just the way that big people do.

For you parents who are teaching your children to bowl with bumpers, encourage them to try to keep their shots from impacting against those artificial barriers. Reserve special praise for shots that would have remained on the lane had bumpers not been present.

Bumpers are great for birthday parties and youth leagues. Because of the damage that would be inflicted due to the velocity of older players' shots, most centers place an age ceiling on who can use them. They also take time to set up, so that they are usually only used for groups with reservations.

That means that Junior is unlikely to be allowed to play with bumpers when bowling with Mom and Dad or during open play. Nevertheless, most kids still have a great time on any occasion when they're treated to a trip to the lanes.

That they enjoy their bowling is the single most significant ingredient that will help them realize their potential. But there are other little instructional tips that should prove helpful.

*The second step toward learning how to bowl is to stand up and toss the ball between your legs.* Dan Chidester

## A LOGICAL TEACHING PROGRESSION

At the stage when your child is still rolling the ball between his or her legs the alignment of the ball's holes is important. Because part of the ball must be removed to drill the holes, a bowling ball's center of gravity may be slightly off center. If the finger holes are to the side as your child rolls his or her shot, the ball is less likely to go straight.

Teach your kid to imagine that the two finger holes and one thumbhole form a triangle. With the thumbhole closest to the foul line, the triangle should point at the headpin. This will allow for the ball to have a more even side-to-side weight distribution so that shots rolled straight are more likely to stay straight.

Children can learn how to push the ball with the same force with both hands and to follow through at their target.

These little lessons serve two purposes. Obviously they will help the youngster bowl better. At the same time, they teach a child how to concentrate. By learning to check the position of the holes on every shot, your kid will be developing memory skills that will later be put to good use as a student.

The progression to placing one's fingers in the ball should not occur until the child is ready to handle a six-pound object with one arm. Usually age five or six is the norm but it all depends on the individual. Don't push a youngster into doing something he or she is not ready to accept.

As when bumpers are removed, children are not likely to become discouraged at lower scores after taking the step from a two-handed to a single-handed release. Most kids will stand sideways at the foul line and swing the ball either well out to the side or behind their back. Either way, very few shots will stay on the lane.

As best you can, help the child to keep his or her hand behind the ball and to be square to the line. Remind him or her that throwing a shot hard isn't nearly as important as rolling it straight. A far shorter armswing that can be controlled is desirable. The concept of utilizing the arrows as targets should be introduced. Your child can learn to stand slightly to the side and roll strike shots over the second arrow and to use the same cross-lane spare strategy as adults do.

In another year or two the child should be ready to use a normal delivery in which he or she takes several steps to the line. The keys here are to slide with the opposite foot and keep the movements slow enough to always be under control.

As your child grows, his or her hand grows too. Periodically check your kid's ball for fit. It's not a difficult proposition for your pro to plug and drill the ball again. Finger holes, thumbholes, and spans that do not fit properly can cause discomfort and will hinder performance.

Just as senior citizens want to feel younger, youngsters

like to feel older. It's natural for kids to want to emulate adult players by throwing a hook ball, using urethane equipment, and going to a fingertip grip.

There's nothing wrong with any of that if the timing is right. As a rule of thumb, I would hold off on urethane while maintaining a conventional grip until at least the teenage years. There is little to be gained and a lot to lose by subjecting developing wrist and forearm muscles to excessive strain.

As important as it is for you to get your equipment drilled by an experienced pro shop owner, it's even more important for your child. Find a pro whose abilities leave you feeling comfortable that there is no danger of a ball that doesn't fit or is too heavy. Failure to do so could result in tendon damage to your child's still developing wrist.

## AMPLE REWARDS FOR THE GIFTED FEW

There are many marvelous junior league programs throughout North America. I know of many fine youth players who have won significant scholarship money toward their college education.

Speaking of that topic, bowling on campus has become a hot growth sport. When I graduated from high school in 1972, college bowling was little more than a nice form of recreation. That's no longer the case. Several of the top schools have excellent teams who travel extensively. There are scholarships available for both males and females.

I can't emphasize more strongly how well advised a gifted 18-year-old would be to get his or her college education first before giving the pro game a try. Every year many optimistic rookies hit the Tour but only a small handful enjoy any appreciable success.

Having something to fall back on is vital. In addition, the pro newcomers with college bowling experience enjoy a competitive edge. They are well traveled and have rolled on a wide variety of lane conditions. Besides all of that, playing a college sport is a lot of fun.

If there's a promising youth bowler in your family, call the Wisconsin-based Young American Bowling Alliance (YABA). They'll be happy to guide your child in the right direction. Their number is (414) 421-4700.

Finally, teach your child the value of maintaining a good attitude. Not only will this provide your youngster with a competitive edge, it will make him or her a better person. If you need a role model to drive home that point, may I suggest Brian Voss, Carol Norman, Rene Fleming, Mike Aulby, and Dave Husted. All of them are models of sportsmanship who exemplify the highest standards even when things don't go their way.

# DAVID OZIO'S 12 PRINCIPLES OF BETTER BOWLING

*1.* To obtain positive results, a positive attitude is positively vital.

*2.* Prior to every shot you must make certain that no foreign object has become attached to the bottom of either shoe.

*3.* Determine your strategy before you step onto the approach.

*4.* Everything starts with a good pushaway, in which the ball is projected forward and toward your target.

*5.* Keep your eyes riveted on your target throughout your entire delivery and until after the ball has rolled past the arrows.

*6.* As in life, proper (consistent) timing is vital.

*7.* Maximum striking power derives from executing a proper release while the ball is still within the leverage window.

*8.* Upon releasing the ball your shoulders must be square (perpendicular) to your target.

*9.* Follow through at your target.

*10.* Your job isn't over on any shot until you have carefully observed how your ball has reacted to the lanes and to the pins so that you can make any necessary adjustments on subsequent deliveries.

*11.* Never forget that ignorance is only blissful to your opponent. Knowledge, confidence, and practice are the keys to good bowling.

*12.* Good luck, and always have fun.

# Glossary

**Arrows:** Series of seven triangular designs 14½–15½ feet past the foul line that are placed every fifth board across the lane to serve as aiming points for shots.

**Axis weight:** Method of ball drilling that decreases hook and produces a rollout effect. Usually used only for ultra-power players. The ball's holes are drilled several inches to the left of the label for a right-handed player (right of the label for a left-handed player) with an extra hole placed in the center of the top weight.

**Back end:** Portion of the lane between the arrows and the pin deck, which consists of softer wood (pine).

**Back pitch:** Angling of thumbhole backward so the tip of the thumb is extended away from the palm. It is used to help the thumb exit the ball sooner to maximize lift. By far the most common of the various thumb pitches.

**Ball sanding:** *See* Sanding.

**Ball shining:** *See* Shining.

**Ball track:** Portion of the ball that comes in contact with the lane as it rolls down the alley. (*See* Spinner, Semi-roller, and Full roller.)

**Bellying:** *See* Deep inside line.

**Blocked lane:** A high-scoring condition whereby the boards closest to the gutters have very little lane conditioner and there is a heavy oil buildup on the center boards, which helps to keep shots in the pocket. If too flagrant it is illegal.

**Boards:** Strips of wood that extend from the start of the approach to the pins. They are used as both a starting and an aiming point by players. There are 39 boards on a lane.

**Carrydown:** Movement of lane conditioner caused by a succession of shots from beyond where the oil was applied toward the pins. It decreases the ball's hooking on the back end.

**Conditioner:** *See* Oil.

**Conventional grip:** Placing one's fingers into the ball up to the second joint. It promotes accuracy but retards lift and striking power. Used primarily by beginning and less advanced players.

**Cranker:** Bowler who relies more on a big hook and great carrying power than on accuracy to succeed.

**Creep speed:** A ball that is rolled very slowly.

**Deep inside line:** A strike line that's popular among big hook players in which the bowler stands on a high-numbered board and aims for a lower-numbered board.

**Dots:** Series of seven spots found seven feet past the foul line, on the foul line, and also at the two most common starting points on the approach. Each dot is on the same board as a corresponding arrow. Their primary function is to provide a reference point for foot placement. They can also be used for aiming points.

**Early timing:** Releasing the shot prior to the sliding foot reaching the foul line.

**Fifth arrow:** The third from the left (for a right-handed player) or from the right (when defined by a left-handed player) of the seven targets painted on the lane. Located on the 25th board.

**Finger grips:** Inserts placed into finger holes of the ball to promote later release for added lift.

**Fingertip grip:** Grip whereby the bowler inserts fingers only up to the first joint. Used to promote hook and striking power at the expense of some accuracy.

**Finger weight:** Drilling of the ball in such a manner that the finger holes are closer to the ball's label than is the thumbhole. It is a form of positive weight. Legal limit is one ounce.

**First arrow:** The farthest to the right (for a right-handed player) or from the left (when defined by a left-handed player) of the seven targets painted on the lane. Located on the fifth board.

**Forward pitch:** Angling of thumbhole inward and/or finger holes upward so the tip of the bowler's thumb is pointing toward the palm and/or the fingers are angled away from the palm. Used for players with small hands and/or short spans to help them grip the ball.

**Fourth arrow:** The target in the middle of the seven targets painted on the lane. Located on the 20th board.

**Full roller:** Method of rolling a ball in which the track area cuts between the thumb and finger holes. While it once was the shot most frequently used, it is rare among better players today because it lacks the carrying power of the more popular semiroller.

**Heads:** Front portion of the lane between the foul line and the arrows, which consists of hard wood (maple).

**Hold area:** Amount of margin for error that is provided by an oil buildup in the center of the lane.

**Hooking lanes:** Dry or lightly oiled condition, which causes maximum hook.

**In time:** Simultaneous arrival at the foul line of one's sliding foot and release of the ball.

**Kickbacks:** Hard walls on both sides of the pin deck used to promote pin deflection so pins ricochet back into play. Also known as *sidewalls.*

**Kill shot:** Shot in which the bowler intentionally reduces the amount the ball will hook.

**Lane conditioner:** *See* Oil.

**Lateral pitch:** Angling of thumbhole and/or finger holes to the left or to the right. Thumb pitch affects exit timing. Angling hole to the left for a right-handed player (or to the right for a left-handed bowler) delays thumb release from the ball, while angling to the opposite direction promotes earlier thumb exit. Improper lateral pitch can cause soreness of the thumb.

**Late timing:** So-called plant-and-shoot method whereby a player releases the shot after the sliding foot has come to a halt.

**Leverage weight:** Method of drilling the ball so that the holes are a few inches to the left of the label for a right-handed player (or to the right of the label for a left-handed bowler). Its effect is to make the ball skid longer and finish stronger. An extra hole is drilled in the opposite side of the ball. The center of the ball's weight block is thus located between the grip and the balance (extra) hole. The fourth hole is required to keep the weight differential within the legal limit of one ounce.

**Leverage window:** Zone in which a shot can be released to gain the greatest assistance from the leg muscles for increased carrying power.

**Lift:** Power imparted to the ball's roll by the thumb exiting the ball first, followed by fingers, hitting through the shot on its release.

**Limited distance dressing (LDD):** *See* Short oil.

**Loading and unloading:** *See* Wristing.

**Loft:** Distance the ball carries after it is released before it hits the lane. When properly executed the shot travels forward, *not* upward or downward.

**Lofting:** To loft one's shot.

**Long oil:** Condition in which oil is applied from the foul line to 35 or more feet of the 60-foot lane. Used primarily for PBA and other highly competitive tournaments to create a challenging condition for the advanced-level player.

**Lustre King:** Machine that applies wax to the surface of bowling balls to prolong ball life and decrease hook.

**Maple:** Hard wood used for that portion of the lane between the foul line and the arrows.

**Negative weight:** Use of one or more drilling methods that decrease the ball's amount of hook and/or gets the ball to end its skid and begin its roll pattern sooner. Primarily employed to combat short oil and/or lightly oiled lanes.

**Oil:** Conditioner applied to a lane's surface that extends life of the alley while retarding ball hook.

**Out of bounds:** Segment of a lane nearest the gutter on certain oil patterns in which an errant shot will be unable to reach the pocket.

**Pin deck:** Portion of the lane housing the pins.

**Pine:** Softer wood used for that portion of the lane between the arrows and the pin deck.

**Pitch:** Angle at which the holes are drilled.

**Play the gutter:** Strike shot angle in which the ball rolls just inside the gutter before it begins its hooking pattern into the pocket.

**Polyester:** Substance used for bowling balls that was very popular among pros in the 1970s and remains commonly used by amateur players. Its effect is a cross between urethane and rubber. A polyester ball goes straighter and doesn't hit as well as a urethane ball but hooks more and hits harder than a rubber one. Preferred by advanced-level bowlers where the lanes are exceedingly dry.

**Polyurethane:** *See* Urethane.

**Positive weight:** Use of one or more drilling methods that increase the ball's amount of hook and/or get it to conclude its skid and begin its roll pattern late. It is primarily employed to combat long oil and/or heavily oiled lanes.

**Power player:** *See* Cranker.

**Reverse block:** Extremely difficult lane condition in which the boards nearest the gutters are heavily oiled while the lane's center is relatively dry.

**Reverse pitch:** *See* Back pitch.

**Revolutions:** The number of times the bowling ball rolls over its circumference from when it is released until it reaches the pins. The greater the number, the more striking power usually results. Higher-quality amateur players and strokers usually achieve 10–20 revolutions. The PBA Tour's ultra-power players are usually in the 15–20 range on their strike shots.

**Revs:** *See* Revolutions.

**Ringing 7-pin:** Tap suffered by a left-handed player when the 4 pin flies around the 7 pin.

**Ringing 10-pin:** Tap suffered by a right-handed player when the 6 pin flies around the 10 pin.

**Rocket speed:** A ball that is rolled very fast.

**Rollout:** Malady in which the ball uses up most of its impetus early on so little carrying power remains by the time it reaches the pins. The shot will actually stop its hooking pattern as it approaches the pins.

**Rubber:** Bowling ball surface that remains the most common among house balls. Rubber bowling balls were the balls of choice well into the 1970s until polyester balls were introduced. Rubber balls go straightest and may be useful for covering non-double-wood spares when decreasing hook is necessary on a very dry lane. Very rarely used by advanced players.

**Sanding:** Using an abrasive substance against the entire surface of the ball. The effect is to get the ball to hook more.

**Second arrow:** The second from the right (for a right-handed player) or from the left (when defined by a left-handed player) of the seven targets painted on the lane. Located on the 10th board.

**Semifingertip grip:** Grip in which player inserts fingers into the ball halfway between the first and second joints.

**Semiroller:** Most popular shot among better-quality players in which the ball's track area can be found just outside of the thumb and finger holes.

**Seventh arrow:** The farthest to the left (for a right-handed player) or to the right (when defined by a left-handed player) of the seven targets painted on the lane. Located on the 35th board.

**Shining:** Adding wax to a ball's surface to make it smoother. Used to retard hook and/or extend ball life.

**Short oil:** Also known as *limited distance dressing* (or LDD). Condition in which oil is applied to the front 24 feet (or less) of the lane, thus leaving the final 36 feet (or more) dry.

**Shur-Hook:** Cork substance used in thumbhole to promote better grip. Commonly used by the player who wants to maintain a similar feel when switching bowling balls.

**Sidewalls:** Walls to either side of the pin deck off which the pins can ricochet back into play. Also known as *kickbacks.*

**Sixth arrow:** The second from the left (for a right-handed player) or from the right (when defined by a left-handed player) of the seven targets painted on the lane. Located on the 30th board.

**Soft 7-pin:** Shot by a left-handed player on which the 7 pin remains as the 4 pin falls weakly into the gutter. Caused by the ball deflecting to the left after colliding with the headpin.

**Soft 10-pin:** Shot by a right-handed player on which the 10 pin remains as the 6 pin falls weakly into the gutter. Caused by the ball deflecting to the right after it collides with the headpin.

**Solid 7-pin:** *See* Ringing 7-pin.

**Solid 10-pin:** *See* Ringing 10-pin.

**Spinner:** Method of delivering a shot so that only a small portion of the ball (around the 7 o'clock position for right-handers and 5 o'clock for lefties) is in contact with the lane. As a rule this is not a very successful shot for maximizing carrying power and thus is rarely employed by the better-quality bowler.

**Straight player:** Bowler who places a premium on accuracy at the expense of power.

**Stroker:** *See* Tweener.

**Suitcase grip:** Holding the ball like the handle of a suitcase to reduce the amount it will hook.

**Swing area:** Amount of margin for error to the right of a right-handed player's target (or to the left of a left-handed player's target) that is provided by a lack of conditioner on the lowest numbered boards.

**Tap:** A single-pin leave on a shot that could have carried.

**Third arrow:** The third from the right (for a right-handed player) or from the left (when defined by a left-handed player) of the seven targets painted on the lane. Located on the 15th board.

**Three-quarter roller:** *See* Semiroller.

**Thumb grips:** Inserts placed inside thumbhole to help player get a better grip. Used primarily to maintain the same feel when player switches bowling balls.

**Thumb weight:** Method of drilling ball so the thumbhole is closer to the label than are the finger holes. It is a form of negative weight that causes the ball to roll sooner. Maximum legal limit is one ounce.

**Tight lanes:** Heavy and/or long oil pattern that retards a shot's hook.

**Timing:** Relationship between the sliding foot and the hand that releases the shot. (*See* Early timing *and* Late timing.)

**Top weight:** Drilling of ball so that there is up to the maximum legally allowed limit of three ounces more of weight above the label than there is below it. Effect on shot is similar to positive weight.

**Track:** *See* Ball track.

**Tweener:** Player who has more accuracy but less power than a cranker and less accuracy but more power than a straight shooter.

**Twister:** *See* Cranker.

**Urethane:** Surface substance introduced in bowling balls in early 1980s. Considered state-of-the-art equipment that is noted for its superior gripping of the lane coupled with maximum carrying power.

**Walled lane:** *See* Blocked lane.

**Walls:** *See* Kickbacks.

**Washout:** Spare leave involving the headpin (and possibly other pins to its left) in combination with the 10 pin (for right-handed players) or the headpin (and possibly other pins to its right) in combination with the 7 pin (for left-handed players). Not considered a split.

**Weight block:** Added section of weight on the inside of the ball. Can be used to maximum advantage by skilled ball driller when placed off center. (*See* Axis weight, Back pitch, Finger weight, Forward pitch, Lateral pitch, Leverage weight, Negative weight, Positive weight, Thumb weight, *and* Top weight.)

**Wristing:** Method of increasing carrying power by altering the angle of the wrist from a cupped to a flat position during a shot's release.

# Index